"A healing journey for anyone who have lost parents or still have parents."

"Friendship is long sort, rarely found and with difficulty kept." So I knew my Friend's heart was broken when he lost his parents....I encouraged him to share his expression of understanding and love that will take us all on a universal journey of healing we can identify with. Whether it is the lost of a parent, child, good friend or someone you valued.....this expression will help to begin the healing....Your Beloved Friend....Queen Lawanda

When I Lost My Parents
A Memoir by Tirlok Malik

*"My loving Mother gave me Wings and
My Father taught me to Fly"*

AuthorHouse™ LLC
1663 Liberty Drive
Bloomington, IN 47403
www.authorhouse.com
Phone: 1-800-839-8640

Published by AuthorHouse 07/08/2014

ISBN: 978-1-4969-1674-7 (sc)
ISBN: 978-1-4969-1673-0 (e)

Library of Congress Control Number: 2014911122

Dedicated to:

Tara and Amrit Malik

My loving Mother who gave me wings,
&
My brave Father who taught me to fly.

When I Lost My Parents
A Memoir By Tirlok Malik

The author Tirlok Malik says, "I was considered successful and mature, but when I was faced with the dilemma of losing my parents, inside I felt I was a small boy who was sacred by the thought of losing my parents."

This book prepares you for that moment when you face the reality of losing your aging parents.

This book is a healing journey for anyone who have lost parents or who still has parents.

CONTENTS

Acknowledgements

Over the years I have met many people from all walks of life and all nationalities.

Some of them have taught me things, some of them gave me love, some of them showed me their kindness, and some of them caused me pain as well.

I thank all of them for making me grow.

I thank all my friends who have stood by me like angels during my times of need.

I thank all my well wishers, you know who you are.

I thank my family for being a part of my journey.

As well as my friends who helped me with this book

I especially thank Tita Beal and Jordan Barsky for double-checking my Indian American English.

Wishing everyone the best in all aspects of life,

Tirlok Malik

Why Did I Write This Memoir?

I was considered successful and mature, but when I was faced with the dilemma of losing my mother, inside I felt I was a small boy who was scared by the thought of losing my mother. When parents are at that stage where they could die, you as a child become the parent and they become the child. I was lonely and scared. I needed an outlet for what I was feeling so I started to write this. When I finished in 2006, I felt healed.

Only much later, some friends read what I had written and said I should share this with others because the feelings are universal and it could be helpful for others as well.

Tirlok Malik

Why should you read this book?

To live life fully, we often need the courage to look directly at our fear of loss.

If your parents are still on the planet, you may not want to imagine their deaths. Tirlok Malik's story reminds us to use our time together fully – to resolve breaks

If you have faced loss of parents or other loved ones, this book is healing as Malik has the courage to work through the pain to the beauty in our moments of connection… even when those moments may include the need to re-connect.

As I took the journey in this book, I followed Malik's path through the anguish of saying goodbye to a courageous and joyful celebration of life.

--Tita Theodora Beal, a reader who, like you, came onto this planet through parents

INTRODUCTION

It was a Friday evening, December 12, 2003. I walked into the restaurant (Ayurveda Café). My mother, Tara, was sitting at her regular table. She looked at me and smiled gently.

I asked her, "Kaya hal hai? Bibi" (How are you, mother.)

She extended her hand to me, "Look what has happened. I get tired after walking one block."

I saw her hand was swollen. I took her hand in my hand, put my other hand on top of hers, looking straight at her and said, "I will take you to the doctor. It will be okay."

While I was looking into her eyes, I realized our roles have been reversed.

All these years whenever anything happened to me, I would tell her and she would respond by saying, "Don't worry everything will be okay. God will bless you" and I believed her every time, no matter what was the outcome. Just merely listening to her say that everything will be okay, I felt everything will be okay. Her words to me were like God speaking. She represented to me the form of God. But that evening when I looked at her face, I realized she has become old and now I will have to be the parent.

On Dec. 15th, Monday, my father Amrit and I took my mother Tara to her regular doctor and setup appointments with other doctors for various tests to be done during the week. After the doctor visit, I took her to see the new restaurant our group was opening. So that she could give her blessings to the new restaurant.

After various tests on December 18th, which was a Thursday afternoon, we were in the cardiologist's office on Central Park West. After doing her checkup, the doctor called me to his office while she was in the waiting room. The doctor informed me that she needed to be taken to the emergency room in the hospital. He said her heart valves were not functioning properly, and liquid had been collecting in her lungs causing her swelling. He said he had called the ambulance already.

I went into the other room and informed my mother that we will have to go to the hospital. She said, "I don't want to go to the hospital."

I extended my hand, touched her face and said, "Mother, in order to get better, we will have to take you to hospital. Don't worry, it will be okay."

While we are waiting for the ambulance, she takes off her gold jewelry and hands it over to me, saying, "Keep it safe." Then she also says she has made four gold bangles for my wife to-be. Those bangles are lying in her bank locker.

Why did she mention this to me at that time? I said, "Don't worry, you will give them to her whenever the time comes."

She said, "Yes, whenever..."

While my father and I were waiting for the ambulance to come, I was looking at my mother's face and realized I have never ever seen her sick before. She is 78 years old.

We reached the emergency room at Lenox Hill hospital at 6:30 PM. They attended to her immediately; we were there till 1:00 in the morning. For dinner, I brought some fruit for her. She shared part of the fruit with my father and joked around with him. She was in good spirits. The doctors were going to keep her the whole night in the emergency room. She told us to go home.

Next morning, my father and I went to the hospital. She was still in the emergency room and she looked fine. She told me she already had breakfast. Sometime later she was given a room on the regular floor. They were going to keep her a few days in the hospital.

During the day, my brother Chander and one of our partners, Bansal, visited her. (My parents treated Bansal like a son.) We spent most of the day in the hospital. Around 8:00 PM, visiting hours were over on the general floor so we all left and went to a restaurant for dinner.

After dinner my father went home while the rest of us stayed at the restaurant. Around 10:00 PM I called hospital and spoke to the nursing station on her floor. The nurse informed me that my mother was restless and she took off the I.V. tubes. We all went back to the hospital and explained to my mother not to take the tubes off. She agreed, and then we all left around 1:00 AM.

Next morning, Mr. Bansal went to the hospital first. When he got there, she was sleeping and he did not wake her up. He sat in her room and watched her. After a while he noticed there was no movement in her for sometime; he informed the nursing station.

A doctor came to see her and informed the nursing station immediately, saying "CODE BLUE 7." The team of doctors came rushing into the room and she was put on machines and I.V. tubes. She was unconscious. The doctors discovered that carbon dioxide was building inside her. While the doctors were doing their work, we all came: Chander, his wife Karen, my father and I.

I saw her lying unconscious with all machines and tubes. In my private movements, the little boy in me was very scared and frightened - what If Mr.Bansal had not noticed she was not moving...

I saw Chander sitting on floor, looking at her, tears in his eyes. I know his love for our mother. My father went inside her hospital room, came out with tears. Then he went back in, came out again.

"No, she cannot go like this. She has to get better - she is going to come home," my father said. Then he added, "Listen, I understand it will affect you if anything happens to her but just imagine how it will affect me, my life. She *is* my life."

He said he was firm and not "shaking" inside. He suggested we have faith in God. "God will do what is right for your mother. I understand it is natural to feel scared but you must surrender her well-being to god and let doctors do what needs to be done." He further said, "Once you surrender to God, don't bring fear inside yourself. Even though it is natural to feel afraid, don't try to live in it, feel it. Just throw it back to God. Because God knows better - your thinking can be wrong, but He cannot be wrong." He repeated, "God will do what's right for her."

I looked at my father compassionately, while listening to him. I saw no fear in his face; instead I saw faith and hope. I have known my father to be a very spiritual man. My mother is the only woman my father has known for 60 years and they love each other. At that moment I chose to plug-in to his faith and hope and then I informed my elder brother in Canada and as well as my sister in India.

The next day, my mother was moved to seventh floor in ICU (Intensive Care Unit). She began to improve a little but still not out of danger. Nurses were taking care of her. My mother spoke no English so I wrote a chart translating English words such as "pain, where, yes, no, water, comfortable, relax, are you breathing," etc. in Hindi (a language my mother, who spoke Punjabi, could understand.) I made photocopies of the chart, gave them to the nursing station and also pasted one next to my mother's bed. I did this so that the nurses could communicate with my mother in the night when we were not there.

At night in my apartment, I tried to sleep, but could not. I felt there were thousands of needles pinching my back. I was wondering, was she comfortable in the hospital? What might she be thinking? Is she scared? Before going to bed I did call the nursing station and asked how she was. The nurse replied, "Your mother is stable and she is sleeping."

In the early morning, when I woke up I called the hospital to inquire about her condition. I was informed she was stable and awake. I remembered an incident in my childhood once I fell from a height and was sick; my mother stayed awake all nights watching over me. That's what mothers do.

I asked for a letter from the hospital about the condition of my mother and, along with some other information, sent it to my sister in India so that she could get a visa to come to see mother. I know my sister Niru had a very, very special relationship with mother. My parents lovingly called her "Guddi" (which means "doll.") I was praying that she should get the visa in time because the US Embassy in Delhi was going to be closed for Christmas holidays. I knew how disturbed emotionally my sister was about the condition of mother and she wanted to come to see her.

My mother's condition was very much improving. She was fully conscious and aware of her surroundings. A friend of mine, Dr. Nara came to visit my mother in the hospital, spoke to her Nurse, looked at her chart, and said, "She will be fine. She will come home and you will see her walking with your father on Broadway." I felt very hopeful; I thanked all the nurses and doctors for taking care of my mother.

On Dec. 23rd, my mother was moved to ICU's step down section on the same floor in a room with another Indian lady patient. They both spoke to each other in Hindi. She translated for my mother to the nurse in the night when we were not there. The next day the Indian lady said to me, "Your mother and I have become sisters. She is a wonderful lady." We all were very happy to know that she was out of danger. The social worker spoke to me to work out a plan for discharging my mother in few days.

My mother began to get better in the hospital. I asked my mother should I invite sister to come visit she said, "Not yet. Let me get better." She did not know my sister was coming and I did not tell her. Around Thanksgiving at my brother's house, the whole family and some close friends get together every year to celebrate that time. We each pick a slip from a box and whoever's name you got on the slip, you buy a gift for that person without telling anyone. At Christmas time, we would put these presents around the tree. Each person would open their present and it was a surprise, basically, not a formality - it's for fun - each person buys one gift and gets one gift. For kids it's different; everybody buys for the kids.

This year, when I picked the slip, I was supposed to buy a gift for my mother. I wanted to bring my sister as a Christmas gift to my mother. The day before Christmas Eve, I said to my mother, "I will bring the Christmas gift tomorrow."

She said, "No I will take it from you when I come home."

My sister got the visa but could not fly on Dec. 24th from Delhi because there was fog at the airport and the flight was cancelled.

Dec. 25th, on Christmas Day, we all came to visit my mother in the hospital, bringing the gifts and flowers. We celebrated Christmas in her room. She was very happy to see everybody, including my brother's children. My mother was really looking good. I said, "Thank God, we are going to take her home soon." Afterwards all she would have to do was take two pills in the morning and two in the evening to keep her condition stable.

On Dec. 26th I went to the airport and brought my sister to the hospital. I told my sister to wait outside and I went to the nurse and explained my sister has come. I wanted the nurse to know just in case, because my mother's heartbeat could become irregular with all of the extra excitement. I went in the room while my sister waited outside I said to my mother should I invite sister to visit? And my mother had such a smile - like a kid smiling.

"Is Guddi here?" she asked, and the smile on her face said everything. I knew she knew. I don't know how she knew that my sister was there on the same floor. I said yes.

The smile - when my sister came into the room and she gave a hug to my mother – the smile was beautiful. A Kodak moment. A smile beyond words. It was one of those moments you have to see; you can't capture it. You just have to feel it. It's like seeing a person that you love - your heart palpitates. It could be your child, or someone that you love. An innocent smile that was so pure.

The next day my sister washed mother's hair with the special care, using dry shampoo. My mother sat on the chair and they talked about lot of things. My sister was staying with me and we would talk at home. I have always known my sister to be like a second mother to me since I came to this country. I have such a relationship with my sister - I mean I can talk to her about anything - she can tell me anything. I felt emotionally supported by her during the time and I needed that.

December 28th: Mother was feeling well and improving very much. She was stable and talking. We were having the grand opening of a new restaurant that evening. I said to my mother, "I'm going to take my sister to the opening of the restaurant."

Mother said, "Sure, show her the restaurant, and take her there."

Then I looked at my father and joked with my mother: "Shall I take the Father, too?"

She looked at me and said, "I don't have a chain around his neck!" I laughed very loud. I liked her making this joke because it made me feel that she was getting her sense of humor back. She also said to give her best wishes for success to everyone there at the restaurant, workers and partners. We went to the restaurant enjoyed the opening and came back to see Mother along with friends and partners. They brought flowers and came to seek her blessings personally. It was great.

I was surprised when three of the employees on the ICU floor told me if they ever get seriously sick they would not seek medical help at Lenox Hill Hospital. I wondered why? I soon found out.

On the morning of December 30th, my mother informed us that she was having pain in her stomach. I and my sister both asked the nurses who said they knew about it and would have a sonogram done on her. They already had her on the list. My mother was in pain and I kept telling her to hold on, to bear with the pain because they don't know what is causing it. They cannot do anything until they know what the causes are.

I went to the ICU (Intensive Care Unit) and asked a doctor to come and see her. The doctor thought it might be a kidney stone or may be something else. I asked the nurses at least five times, "Please do something soon - she is in pain."

The nurse said, "She is in ICU that means Intensive Care."

I said, "No she isn't in ICU - this is a step down from ICU." I was surprised at the nurse. I had just finished listening to her on the phone talking to somebody on what seemed like a personal phone call.

The nurse said, "Tara's name is on the list. Monday is a busy day and they take people by priority. There might be lot of people in the emergency room." I asked her to please do something soon.

Then I saw Barbara, the administrator for 7th floor. Barbara said, "We know the family always feels more concerned, but we are aware and will take care of it."

"But she is in pain!" I said. Barbara said she understood.

Around 4 o'clock they took the sonogram but found nothing. They couldn't really see anything. At that point they decided to do a cat scan and in order for them to do a cat scan you have to wait two hours after drinking some liquid. Around 7:00 PM they did the Cat Scan and they found she was bleeding inside. It's called hematoma. She was brought back immediately to the ICU again. That night my sister stayed in the hospital with Mother in her room.

I felt very badly and thought I should have created a big scene with the nurse and the doctor. I should not have listened to the nurse and Barbara when they said that they were aware of the pain of my mother and they would take care of it.

I have always believed that the doctors and nurses know what they are doing in the hospital. I looked towards them like they are the form of God because they can save patients and at the same time I, like most people, was afraid to create a fight with the medical staff, especially when they are taking care your loved one. I have always wondered when something like this happens, is it the human errors or the destiny of the patient?

Next morning the doctor explains to me what a hematoma is and that they have to wait for it to go away. They cannot do the drainage; it might cause her to have an infection. So, they had to wait and see. In the meantime, they cannot give her blood thinners because it might increase the bleeding. But if no blood thinners, she might risk having a stroke. It was a very unfortunate situation. I felt very numb. There was nothing we could do, except wait and see. My mother's doctor also wanted to have a non-aggressive approach because she was old. His feeling was that if they touch something it might open other things and create more problems.

I spoke with doctors outside the hospital. Other doctors said you could drain it and risk the infection - and give some other medicine to control the infection. You cannot tell a doctor what to do. You should not because they know better. At least you hope for that. A doctor friend also told me most likely it is possible that bleeding may have been caused by giving the injection the wrong way in the stomach while giving her blood thinner. The injection might have punctured a vein in her stomach and that may have caused the bleeding. But it is very hard to prove that.

I discussed the treatment given to my mother with two other friends who are doctors working in New York hospitals. They are very accomplished doctors. They did not think the doctor gave the right treatment to my mother. One doctor also told me sometimes hospitals will do a simple procedure in such a manner so that they can justify it to the insurance company - in order to get paid more.

December 31st, 2003, New Year's Eve: Chander, Karen, Bansal, and some other friends, were in the hospital for most of the day. In the evening, my sister, my father and I stayed back. It was around 8:30 PM. I was discussing with my sister the New Year's Eve party at the Indian Café that we have been having for more than the last 15 years. Chander hosts the party where all our employees from the restaurants, friends and all family members of our partners get together to celebrate the coming of the New Year. We all dine, drink and dance full blast to the music till the morning hours. My parents have attended the party for last 15 years. They love dancing. Everybody would dance with my mother and father and take photographs with them.

This will be the first year when my mother will not be there. I myself don't feel like going to the party. I can go home and have few glasses of wine and knock myself out and go to sleep. The emotional pain is so unbearable that the only thing I can bring myself to do is get drunk and go to sleep. My sister wanted to stay with mother that night and she suggested I should take my father to the party.

My father and I went to the party. People were dancing and enjoying themselves. People did not know that my mother was in the hospital. I did not tell them because I did not want to spoil anyone's mood. I sat at the bar on the last stool in the corner, drinking wine. The whole party looked very colorless to me. My father was trying to dance on the floor and I noticed he was forcing himself. There was no life in his dance. He seemed a lonely man missing his wife. Before this he always loved to dance. He did not care if he knew the music or if he was dancing with somebody. He was very happy dancing solo. Watching him that night broke my heart inside and I did not know what could I do. I did not stay too long that night and I went home. I dropped my father at his home on the way. I was alone and feeling very alone and lost.

On New Year's Day, 2004 I told my mother I missed her last evening at the party and many people asked about her. She said, "You should enjoy", and she smiled. As time went by, she was improving every day even though I did not know what was going to happen. It was a week full of restlessness. Mother was improving; blood from the hematoma was being drained. Father would come by bus on his own and would stay most of the day. He was still very strong in his faith, believing God will do what's right for her.

When she was getting well I remember feeding her fruit, three different kinds of melons. She asked what kinds of melon were they? She said the first and second one she liked but not the third one. I felt good giving her fruit and it was nice to see her eating. At that point one of our partners, Andre from the restaurant Café Con Leche, came in and my mother asked about his children. He was amazed that she would ask about his children before he could ask how she was doing. He said he had a gift for her that he would bring it the next day. My mother said, "No I will get it from you myself when I come to Cafe Leche." That was a good sign. She also said she liked the juice from Café Leche. She never called it Café Con Leche, she called Café Leche.

January 8th 2004, Friday: My mother had a stroke because they were not giving her any blood thinner. The reason for not giving the blood thinner was, her hematoma was being drained. She had a stroke in her brain on the left side, so she was not able to move the left hand and left leg. She was also not able to speak. The stroke affected her speech.

What a disaster... I was at the hospital when they gave me this news. They did not know when it happened. They had to put oxygen tubes in her again. That meant they had to put her on the respirator to help her breathe. That is not good news because when your body cannot breathe on its own, there is a major problem.

Words can hit more sharply than needles. I was talking to Barbara, the 7th floor Administrator, about the process of getting a patient off the ventilator. I said to her I hoped that my mother can get off the ventilator. She got aggressive - almost angry - and said, "What? You are going to get her new lungs? Her lungs are strong enough!" I told her gently, "are we now playing God?" She did not reply.

My mother was off the ventilator for three months before she passed away. Thank you Barbara for playing God. One must choose words carefully. She could have said, "Mr. Malik, medically, it doesn't look like your mother will be able to get off the ventilator but let's hope for the best"

Once in conversation, Barbara told me hospitals in America are run by Wall Street. Barbara is also the woman who, on December 29th 2003 when my mother was waiting for the medical attention, said to me that the family always worries more than necessary: "Mr. Malik, don't worry, we have her name on the list for a checkup." It was on that day, she did not get medical attention in proper time, my mother was bleeding inside more than if she had been checked. Things had begun to go wrong way from that day on.

After her stroke, the doctor said they would start to give her blood thinner which will be supervised. He said there was a chance that during the procedure my mother would experience internal bleeding. The doctor said that if that did happen, my mother's situation would be out of his control. That was a very, very scary feeling to know and I was praying to God to please take care of her and watch over her. They gave her blood thinner everyday and thank God she did not have any complications. The hematoma was drained and thank God nothing went wrong.

I would be sitting in her room and I would look into her eyes. Sometimes she would not take her eyes off of mine. Our eyes were locked. It felt like when someone looks right *into* you. I felt connected. I don't know what we said to each other but we said something. She smiled at me and I would tell her, "I love you." She would smile back and touch my head.

A few days later my sister insisted that I should go to office for few hours. I went to my office and tried to work but couldn't. In the evening my sister called from the hospital to tell me mother was okay and I did not have to come back to the hospital. I told my sister that I would be coming back and I have to see her. I couldn't go to sleep without seeing her. My mother knows I have to come there to say good night. She knows that when I leave I touch her feet and ask if it is okay then to go home and she always says, "Yes, go home. I will see you tomorrow." I told my sister that you may not understand this but I have to see her in the evening and say goodnight. I went to see her in the hospital.

Every night when I am home, I call the nurse to make sure Mother is relaxed and stable, not agitated. I would also thank the nurse very much for taking care of her. I never know what to expect the next day when I will walk into her room.

At home one night I was having dinner and I started thinking about my mother, the image of her being in the hospital lying in bed with the mask on her face… It looked as if she was about to cry because it hurt so much. I wonder what she would have done if she had seen me that way. After that I couldn't finish eating my food.

Next day I went to hospital. She's looking better, more alert. I told her that we all are waiting for her to get well and that she is getting well. She smiles and makes a gesture by her right hand to her mouth. I ask her if she wants eat something. She shakes her head, gesturing No and points her finger towards to me, motioning with her hand. She is asking about my eating habits. She touches my face. I'm surprised. How does she know I am not eating? I say to her, "Yes, I am eating." This is where you have to believe there are invisible strings attached between a mother and a child. A mother can feel her children's pain and happiness. All mothers have this power about the children.

I am sitting alone in the room with her in the morning, very quiet. These times have a very heart wrenching effect on me when I see her there. I said to myself, this woman doesn't say anything but I know what she could be going through. And at that moment I wish I had the healing magic. I could touch her and heal her---just extend my hand out to her and say, "Okay let's go, you are walking home."

My parents lived on 99th Street between Broadway and Amsterdam Avenue in New York City. My Brothers and I got them their own apartment, rather than having to live with one of us since they came to America in 1988. This way they had their own freedom and personal life. They have been living very happily. It was like their second golden Honeymoon. We all lived close by within walking distance.

At the hospital in the waiting room my father told me, tomorrow morning he will not be home; he will be at the Laundromat. I should not worry when I call him in the morning if he is not at home. I said to him, "I will get your laundry done." He said, no he will do it. Before, he used to accompany my mother to the Laundromat. He further said he would do the laundry when she comes home. He will take care of all housework and everything; I looked at him and gave him a hug. I said to him to do only as much as he can and not to carry too much. He said he would not.

I looked at this man who has never even made a cup of tea for himself, and now he is saying of these things.

"I HAVE MOTHER"

One day I was sitting in my mother's room and just thinking about all that was happening. I felt a mother is the most precious gift one can have. An Indian movie, "Deewar" directed by Yash Chopra with Amitab Bachchan and Shashi Kapoor, has a scene with two brothers; they meet in the place where they grew up homeless. Now one brother has become very rich, powerful gangster and the other brother is a police inspector living at home with their mother. In the scene, both brothers are confronting each other.

The gangster brother speaks: "We both grew up in this place and look what I have today: buildings, cars, money, power. And what do you have?"

The other brother is quiet, and then says, "I have Mother."

As I thought about this scene (written by Salim Khan and Javed Akhtar), I thought, how true it is.

The wealth of the whole world or the mother, which one would you chose?

HOSPITAL JOURNEY

Moments from the days, weeks, and months spent in hospitals and rehab clinics flood back:

January 17th 2004, mother was not feeling too well. These days it's a dilemma, not knowing what will happen to my mother. My sister said to me, "You should not put chains of your love onto mother. When our love is very strong in a cosmic way we can hold them in limbo. Let God do what is right for her."

One day, I asked my mother if she wanted to go to God. She pointed her hand upward, suggesting it's up to God. I asked her if she wanted to get better and come home, she signaled "yes". One day, I was very sad, not understanding what was happening and how to deal with it. My sister reminded me what Lord Krishna has said in "Gita". He has said, soul never dies. Knowing philosophy did not ease my pain at that time.

PRIMARY DOCTOR GOES ON VACATION WITHOUT TELLING YOU

In the month of February 2004, my mother's primary doctor left for vacation without telling me. When I did not see him for three days, I asked someone in the ICU room, "Where is my mother's doctor? I have not seen him. I want to speak with him."

I was told that he was not coming in for the next seven days, but I can speak to the attending doctor. I was shocked: how can he do this? Upon his return, I asked him, "Why did you not tell me that you were going on vacation?" He said he told somebody who was sitting in my mother's room when he came to see her before he went to vacation. I said, "You or your office should have called me. You have my number." He did not reply.

I sense for some of these doctors it's about money. The more patients they have, the more money they make. They will sign in, spend five minutes on patient chart, and get paid.

ONE OF THOSE DAYS JANUARY 27TH 2004

I saw my mother - she looked very tired and little lost. That day she touched all family members who came there, Father, Chander, Karen, Sister, Bansal, Sushil, etc. At one time she also folded her hands like "Namasthe," gesturing good-bye. Once she held my sister's hand and then put her hand into mine. As if she was telling me to take care of my sister. I saw tears in her eyes many times that day. I asked her if she wanted to go to God; she gestured 'yes' by nodding her head.

I don't really know what she means; she cannot speak because of the breathing tubes in her mouth. I saw my father crying several times that day. In the evening I had a conversation with my father. It sounded like he was reassuring himself as well. "Not to lose faith," he said, "Let us see what God does. Have faith in God. If God wants her, no doctor will be able to stop that. If God wants to cure her, he will. Let Doctors do their work."

I DREAMED ON FEB 16TH 2004 MOTHER WAS DANCING

On 16th of February I dreamed that mother was dancing with all of us at a function. Next day, in the evening in my mother's room in the ICU, in the presence of my brother Chander, my sister and Mr. Bansal, I told them about my dream. They said, the same day in the afternoon, mother was watching exercise class on TV. Chander and Bansal were talking to mother about her dancing. I hope it was a good omen. My parents loved dancing. They danced on many occasions. Do dreams have any meaning?

FEBRUARY 22nd 2004 - SISTER GOING BACK TO INDIA

My sister has been in New York for almost two months. Now it was the time for her to go back to New Delhi because she was needed there; her daughter-in-law was about to have a baby. My sister had already informed my mother and asked for her permission to go back. My mother was okay with it. My mother, sister and I held hands together and cried.

My sister said, "Bibi (Mother), I will be back and you will get better." My mother had a very special relationship with my sister. Traditionally speaking in India all mothers have a special relationship with their daughter. I told my mother I paid for her ticket. My brothers and I had given her several things to take home. My mother was happy to see us do that. I did not want her to feel just because she was sick, things were not being taken care of. Even though my sister never expected anything, I felt happiness from this tradition. It is a tradition in the Indian culture when a girl comes to her parents' house, parents pay for her traveling, etc.   My sister spent the rest of the day with my mother. Later in the day she left for India. I wondered if my sister will ever see mother again.

LOOKING INTO THE EYES OF MOTHER ON FEBRUARY 28TH 2004

For all this time, any time I look into my mother's eyes, she would look back into my eyes, and communicate. Sometimes she would smile and sometimes she would make a gesture. Sometimes our eyes were locked. But now after the stroke and all these procedures, I saw a change in her eyes. Now her eyes are blank. She has a lost look. When I look into her eyes now she quickly looks the other way. I get a sense she is sad inside and does not want me to see it… or maybe I don't know what it means.

FASHION SHOW - MARCH 2004

One day, I was sitting in my mother's room in the Intensive Care Unit (ICU). My sister was there also. I received a phone call for me to be a model in a fashion show to be held in the Plaza Hotel. My sister said to me, "Do it, its good for you. It's also a part of life." She suggested I should start bringing balance between work and my duty in my life. I took the blessings of father and mother. I did the show. After the show I showed the photographs to my mother. She smiled, happy to see to see pictures of her son.

LIFE ON THE 7TH FLOOR ICU

When your loved one is in ICU for some time, you begin to spend lot of time in the waiting room on the ICU floor as well. There you encounter many other people whose loved ones are on the same floor. You get to know them, observe them, and share feelings with them. You realize that no matter what your religion, color, culture and nationality, when faced with someone in the hospital or ICU, you have many common feelings with them. Their loved ones may be there for different reasons, but fear, hope, anxiety, concern are the same and common. Each person may deal differently with the emotions but you begin to form caring friendly relationships.

When you are a regular visitor to the hospital, even after few days, the security guards on the ground floor entrance do not ask for your ID card any more.

In my time in January-February 2004 at ICU at Lenox Hill Hospital on the 7th floor, I witnessed many incidents full of care, love., conflict, and emotions. They were all teaching something about life and death. Here are some of the moments I witnessed…

A MARRIAGE CELEBRATION

One day in the afternoon around 5 PM, I saw on one side of ICU waiting room that a table was being set with wine, appetizers, and cheeses. There were about ten men and women, all white Americans, drinking wine and champagne. They were talking to each other. I was sitting on the other side of room along with my sister Niru. One man asked me if I would like to have a glass of wine. I said okay and asked what they were celebrating, while I toasted a glass of wine with him.

He told me he was getting married. His father-in-law is in the ICU room for last 2 days. He introduced me to his wife-to-be. "A priest will be coming and we will be getting married in front of her father." They had known each other for two years. He is a musician and she is a business development director for a film production company.

"Congratulations on the marriage," I said. "Thanks for including me." There was an elderly lady who was drinking and shifting between crying and hugging her daughter, the bride. A few hours later, large bouquets of flowers were brought in and put in the bride's father's room. Her father's room was right across my mother's room. A priest came and he was in her father's room along with all the other people. I did not go into the room. They closed the room with the curtain. The priest was performing the marriage ceremony.

Sometime later around 9 PM, some of them were back in the waiting room. When I left from the hospital they were still drinking and talking.

The next day, I came to see my mother and noticed the room across from hers was empty. There were no flowers and no patient. I asked the nurse what happened to the patient, "Has he been moved to another room?"

"I cannot answer this kind of question," the nurse replied.

Sometime later I came to know he had an incurable disease and the family had decided to pull the plug. It happened late last night.

I felt very sad to know this. It gave me the answer why the marriage happened in the ICU room. It was the wish of the bride that her father could see the wedding and give his blessings to the couple before he died.

I questioned what the universe was trying to teach me. Why had I witnessed this? I had no idea what would happen when I shared a glass of wine with them. My heart was filled with compassion for the family and I prayed for them.

A MOTHER'S WORST NIGHTMARE

One day when I came into the waiting room of the ICU, I saw a lady sitting on the other side of the room reading a book. I said Hello to her and asked what book she was reading. She told me she was reading *"Five People You're Going to Meet in Heaven."*

"What is the book about?" I asked.

"It's about a person who dies and goes to heaven and meets five people," she said. During the conversation I came to know her husband was a sports news writer for a major Television Network. "My husband had cancer at an advanced stage. But it was discovered only two days ago."

Her husband was in the same section of the floor where my mother was. I told her why I was there and about my mother.

The next day around 1 PM in the afternoon, I saw the whole family was there - the woman, her two beautiful teenage daughters, her husband's brother and his mother. The mother must have been in her late 70's, a beautiful but frail-looking woman. She looked in pensive mood. As a courtesy I said "Hello" to all of them.

About half an hour later, they all came back to the waiting room. The teenage daughters were crying. Everybody else was very silent. I went to see my mother and came back to the waiting room few minutes later. I came to know they pulled the plug on their family member. The daughters were crying very much. Their mother was trying to calm them down. The elderly lady was sitting in silence. I looked at her; my heart went out to her. Only a mother could imagine what she might be feeling.

I sat there in silence. Soon they were leaving; I also got up, walking over to the elder lady, I gave her a hug and said, "I am sorry to know this". She accepted my hug and hugged me back. And they left. It had a deep affect on me.

A DAUGHTER MISSING THE MOMENT

I met a Spanish girl in her early thirties in the waiting room. In conversations, I came to know her mother was in ICU and she had cancer. I saw the girl coming for two days to visit her mother. She spoke a lot about her mother. On the second day, in the afternoon, after seeing her mother in the ICU room, she came to the waiting room. She was chatting with me and told me she had a good conversation with her mother. She was going to go downstairs to have a hot cup of coffee.

About twenty minutes later, I saw her crying in the hallway. I asked her what happened. She told me that while she had gone out for a cup of coffee, her mother had passed away. I gave her a hug and asked if I could be of any help to her.

Nobody knows the exact moment of when it will happen.

WERE NOT ABLE TO GET IN TOUCH WITH MOTHER

There was a lady who had come from Boston to see her father. She was in her early forties. Her father was in his seventies. He was in the ICU supported by machines. He himself was a doctor by profession.

Her parents were separated. She was divorced, and had a teenage daughter. At present her mother was away on a cruise for two weeks with her boyfriend. Her parents were divorced for many years. She was feeling frustrated about how to inform her mother. She was not able to get in touch with her. Her father's condition was not looking very good. It was time to pull the plug on the machines that kept him breathing. He had signed his wish for this before he got sick.

In conversation, she told me that she is going to miss her father very much although she did not have a good relationship with him.

"Sit near your father," I suggested. "Hold his hand and tell him all that you feel. You can tell him you love him, you will miss him, and you wished you had a better relationship with him. Anything else you want to tell him. He will hear you even though he is on machines and unconscious."

Later in the day when I saw her she told me she did what I suggested and she felt good. She asked me for a hug and thanked me for the suggestion.

The next day in the evening, she informed me that they have pulled all the life support machines from him and they moved him into another room. They are giving him morphine.

"Now we just have to wait," she said.

"Let's go to his room," I suggested. "We can say a prayer to God to release him and give him peace." We both went to his room. I saw him lying there with his mouth open, unconscious, still breathing and waiting to die.

We both held hands together and said a prayer.

The next morning, he passed away. The daughter told me of her loss as she was finishing up all of the paperwork and details before she went back to Boston. She still had not been able to get in touch with her mother.

A FAMILY IN CONFLICT

I met a Hasidic Jewish family in the waiting room. It was a large family of four brother's children and grandchildren. Their father, a rabbi in his late seventies was very ill when he was brought into the hospital.

The whole family used to come every day. They would take turns so that somebody was always there for 24 hours. They used to bring their kosher food. It seemed like they had turned that one corner of the waiting room into a small home. It was nice to see a loving, caring and large family.

In conversation we all talked about what was going on. They also used to feel up and down like waves, as the patient's condition goes up and down. I know the feeling very well because my family was going through the same feelings.

If one procedure goes well, I will overhear one son informing lot of people, saying the procedure was successful. As the days went by, their father's condition begins to get worse and worse. He was put on machine. He could not breathe on his own. One day the elder son was talking to me. I asked him what the condition of his father was.

"Not good," he said. "I feel helpless. Living on machines is horrible. It's a punishment to the person's body. Nothing more can be done to improve my father's condition." He told me he would like to pull the plug on his father and let him go. But his brothers did not agree. A few days later their father died but he had suffered. Family quarrels are bound to happen in times like this.

It's was a very deep learning experience in the ICU waiting room when other people become the mirror of your own fears of being there. I learned many things while observing and interacting with other people with loved ones in the ICU.

FROM HOPE TO NO HOPE

On December 26th 2003, my mother was stable and a social worker was talking to me about discharging her from the hospital. We all were very hopeful and happy in anticipation of taking Mother home. On December 29th she had the hematoma (Internal Bleeding). She was on Comoden. Her blood vessels had ruptured while Comoden was being injected into her stomach. The injection was probably put in at the wrong angle. She had terrible pain. This is how hematoma happened.

She was not given medical attention till 8.00PM in the evening. Bleeding was discovered only after ten hours; even we had informed the nurse that my mother was having pain in the stomach. She was immediately given nine or ten units of blood. In the evening when they discovered hematoma she was put back into ICU, where she remained.

Since December 26th 2003 after that day, Mother had two strokes (they could not give her blood thinner because of hematoma.) She has been incubated (breathing pipes to supply oxygen) three times. Now she is on a ventilator. Her lungs are weak. She was brought into the hospital for having Congestive Heart Failure and Rapid Heart Beats (a leakage in the valve in the heart.) On December 26th, the doctor said she will have to take two pills in the morning and two in the evening… and she should be okay.

Now six weeks later, she is on ventilator. A patient on ventilator cannot go home. At the time, she was able to breathe ten to twelve hours on her own. At night they would put her back on the ventilator for breathing. The goal was to get her off the ventilator so, she could breathe on her own from 10 hours to 24 hours. The Cardiologist and other specialists at Lenox Hill were convinced that Tara Malik would have more chance to get off the ventilator if a Cardiac Catheterization was performed, and the clot removed - if any were found. Cardiac Catheterization was performed by Sriram S. Iyer, MD, of the Heart& Vascular institute.

Initially when Doctor proposed doing Cardiac Catheterization, my first reaction was No. I spoke to my father; he also said No. It was just a gut feeling not to have it done. I also felt doing the Cardiac Catheterization will not solve the original problem. Also there was danger of anything going wrong. I had the feeling that Mother will come off the ventilator eventually, if some more time is given.

I was thinking like a layman - that if you are getting ready for Olympics, you build up step by step. If my mother is doing 10 hours on her own, it can be increased half-an-hour every day. But in the hospital they expect quick results. This is the impression I got from them. (By the way, my mother did get off the ventilator three months before she passed away, but she never went home. Why? Because after the unsuccessful Cardiac Catheterization things went really wrong with my mother.)

I wish we never would have agreed to do the Cardiac Catheterization. But, the doctor continued to suggest it. So we were in limbo – "Shall we do it or not?" A doctor friend of mine also said, "Don't poke your mother's body any more. Don't do Cardiac Catheterization. It will not help. Let her live gracefully for whatever time God has given her". We searched for a second opinion. After examining my mother for only 5 minutes three doctors (all from the same hospital) suggested yes, she is a candidate for Cardiac Catheterization.

I wondered if any doctor would contradict the opinion of another doctor from the same hospital. Even my mother's primary doctor Lestrino C. Baquiran, who initially said no, later also agreed to the procedure. I do not know why she changed her recommendation. We were still not sure, but the last doctor who came in to speak with us convinced us. He really was a talker. We were still in limbo, ready to do anything that would help Mother get better. We believe doctors know what is best for their patient. We were all convinced.

Father signed his permission to perform the procedure on my mother on February 18th 2004. We were all in Mother's room in the ICU, joking with her. I massaged her face and forehead. I even showed my brother Chander how to give her a face massage, using a paper napkin or sometimes by hand. He also gave her a massage on the face. That day, she was off the ventilator for more than 13 hours. The next day, they were going to do Cardiac Catheterization. I asked myself, am I prepared for everything?

The day of the procedure I came early in the morning so that I could spend some time with her. The procedure was supposed to be done around 2:00 PM; around 11:00 AM Dr. Sriram Iyer came and met with me in the ICU waiting room. He told me he had done the procedure many times. He is very accomplished and he even suggested I should check his credentials on the internet. He is an internationally known researcher, giving lectures all over the world. He explained the procedure he said not to worry, there is no danger.

I felt comfortable knowing all these things about him. He told me he also speaks Hindi. I took him to my mother introduced her. He greeted my mother in the Hindi language. I told her he will be doing her procedure and not to worry. Then he left. I spent some more time with my mother. My sister was also there. Around 1:00 PM, they started to unplug the machines, bed wires, etc. to take my mother to the procedure room. While they were doing it, I saw fear on her face. For a few seconds, I again went into limbo. I comforted her and said not to worry, we all will be outside the operation room. They took her away into the operation room.

A few minutes later, my father, Mr. Bansal, his wife, my brother and his wife came. The operation was supposed to start at 2pm. But the doctor decided to do the operation much earlier. Leaving only my sister and I to see my mother off for what might be her last moments on earth.

While we were all sitting outside of the operation room, I asked everyone to hold hands and do a prayer for the success of the procedure.

After sometime Doctor Iyer came to the waiting room and informed us that she was not responding. At that moment she was unconscious. He wanted to have the permission to check something in her brain. We said go ahead if you think it should be done. He went back into the operating room. We waited. I don't remember exactly how much time; - I think they worked on her for an additional 45 minutes before they took her back to her room. She had had a stroke on the right side of her body in the operating room. Dr. Iyer said he was sorry. That day he had done two procedures in the morning and they were both successful. He said he would see me later. He had to go back to the operating room because three other patients were also scheduled for that day.

I did not say anything. I was shocked and felt very numb. We went to see my mother in her room. She looked like a vegetable. No life, no reaction. She looked half dead. We all were shocked that the procedure had not been successful and had created more problems. Everyone remained quiet mostly for the rest of the day. Everyone must have been thinking how everything had changed from last evening. Last evening they saw her smiling and joking with them and now...

A HEART-BROKEN MAN

My father's health started to decline when mother's Angioplasty operation went wrong. He had become very quiet. One evening, my father told me he was going to stay with me in my apartment. That night he slept only a few feet away from me.

Next morning as he got ready and came out of the bathroom after a shave and shower, I saw a few cuts on his face. I guess he was trembling while he shaved. I felt bad. He told me he had a headache, and he felt his heart was sinking. I called the ambulance and took him to Lenox Hill (the same hospital where my mother was).

In the emergency room, doctors did all checkups on him but could not find anything. My father told the doctors and I that he had not been taking his medicine for epilepsy for a while (my father had epilepsy but for the last 15 years, he had been taking medicine and he had been fine). The doctor said that not taking a medicine for a short time should not do harm since he has been taking it for 15 years. The doctor would start to give him medicine now but it would take about 10 days for the medicine to take effect. My father was admitted to the hospital and would be kept under observation for few days. He was not eating well, nor drinking any liquids. He said, "I don't want to eat or drink." He started talking about leaving this world. He said, "I am going. My time has come. I am going to die". I said to him, "What are you talking about - what is this?" I tried to reason with him but he would not listen. I thought eventually he would get hungry and eat. I spent most of the day trying to convince him to eat. He ate very little, but not enough.

The next day when I was in the hospital, I saw him first then I went to see my mother. Father was on the fourth floor and my mother was on the second floor. My father called my brother Chander and said he was calling to say Good-bye and that he was leaving this world. Then he hung up the phone. My brother came rushing down to the hospital and found me sitting right next to my father. My father had not told my brother that I was there at the hospital. For the next two days my father wouldn't eat and continued to talk about how he was going to die. I tried to reason with him many times but he did not listen. I got very angry at him. I lost my temper, because at times I have seen him being stubborn.

A little later, I asked myself why I gotten angry with him. I felt ashamed. I came to realize my inner child was very scared. I wanted for him to be well and to be there with me to take care of my mother. Only a week before he was giving me courage and moral support. Then it occurred to me that his emotional state of mind, his hope for the recovery of his wife (my mother) had been crushed. He was losing his partner of 60 years. When we first brought my mother into the hospital he was very hopeful about her getting better but now that hope had turned to agony. He had seen her condition getting worse in the hospital. I realized "He is afraid of losing her, just as I am." I remembered him telling me in the first week mother was in the hospital that if anything were to happen to her, his life would be most affected.

He might be feeling guilty for letting the doctors to do the angioplasty – as we all did. He's the one who signed the permission. Initially, he also did not want the procedure to be done. I never asked him whether he was feeling guilty about signing the permission. I was afraid that he may not have thought that way and I did not want to plant the seed of guilt in his mind.

Now his grieving has begun. I know he loves her deeply and he is seeing the danger of losing her. He is watching her suffering. He has told me on few occasions how he is lucky to have her as his wife. She has been there with him in ups and downs. She has been truly his partner for 60 years and enriched his life in many ways. He always told me love is the most powerful thing between a husband and wife, even though many times they have conflicts and fights. A couple should never lose love if they truly love each other.

I understood his dilemma. To avoid grief one must then avoid love and that was not possible for my father. He loved my mother too much to shy away. His world was shattering. He was heart-broken. When your heart breaks in love, you don't feel like living. The doctors who had been dealing with him did not understand what was going on inside my father. They thought it was a psychological problem and wanted to consider admitting him to the psychiatry department. I requested a Hindi-speaking psychiatrist. After waiting four days the hospital did not bother to get my father any psychiatrist at all.

On the fifth day a social worker and three doctors called me in to have a meeting with them. They said, "Well, the psychiatry department has accepted your father and they have a room for him. We can transfer him there tomorrow."

I looked at them and asked them, "Do you remember how you felt the first time your heart was broken? That's what my father is feeling. No, he is not a candidate for your psychiatry department. I will take him home". It's important to understand the emotional state of the patient. My father needed loving care and assurance that he would be okay. I am glad I did not agree with doctors' suggestion to admit my father into the psychiatry ward. There he would have been isolated and even more depressed. Three days later we took him home. He was much better and had begun to eat. I think he was in initial immediate shock about the result of my mother's procedure.

It was overwhelming to have both of my parents in the same hospital, my mother on the second floor, my father on the fourth. We would take Father every day to see mother for a short time. He would change out the hospital gown and into his regular clothes to go to see my mother. We never told our mother that Father was also admitted in the hospital at the same time.

We tried to protect my mother from knowing of my father's state in the hospital. I am not sure if we succeeded, because mother might have been able to sense the truth. But as kids we must try to protect.

AMRIT AND AMRIT

When Father was discharged from the hospital he was given a nurse to live with him for 10 hours a day at his apartment from 8:00 AM to 6:00 PM. I began to search for someone to take care of him in the other hours - someone to live with him in his apartment and be there with him. My brother Chander was 100% supportive of this idea. I placed an ad in the Indian newspaper. I began to interview people on phone. I was not able to find anyone suitable immediately but then I got a phone call from a lady who said she was looking to work in a home where she would feel comfortable. In the conversation for some reason I said the word "Nirankar." The lady asked me, "Are you the son of Amrit and Tara Malik who are part of Nirankari sat sang*?" I said, "Yes" then she said, "No more questions, He is also like a father to me."

*sat sang- religious congregation.

She told me she was also the part of the same sat sang and Amrit and Tara had always treated her like a daughter. Then she told me an anecdote about my parents: once, while she was at sat sang in New Jersey, she needed money for a taxi. My parents gave her more money than she needed and said to her that the money is not to be returned to them. She can never forget that kind gesture of helping her. It was the good karma from my parents. It seemed that she was an angel sent from God at the right time. Her name was also Amrit just like my father's name. She moved into my father's place.

My father was very surprised and happy to see her. She took very good care of my father. She made sure he ate properly. They would have conversations about life, God etc. My father had good companion who was like a daughter to him. My father's health began to improve. She also went to see my mother many times a week. My mother was happy to know that she was staying with my father and taking care of him.

She stayed with my father while he was in and out of the hospital during the oncoming months. She used to say, she would take care of my father as long as she was alive. Little do we know sometimes we say things and we don't know why. After my mother's death, when my father got sick again, he was given 24-hour nurse to stay home with him. But we wanted lady Amrit to continue to live with my father. She was like family. She had her own room in my father's apartment.

Because my father had a 24-hour nurse, Amrit felt she could take a trip to India, which she had been waiting to do for a while. Before leaving, she asked me will she still have a room in my father's apartment when she comes back from India? I told her she will always have a place in my father's apartment. She was very happy to hear that and said, "Thank you, brother."

She went to India in October 2004. After she left, my father asked me when she was coming back. I told him she was still in India. In December 2004 when my father was in the hospital, I got a call from lady Amrit's family that she died in the hospital in Amritsar (INDIA). She was having a surgery. It did not go well and she died. When I got the call, I could not believe it. I cried. I did not tell my father because I did not want to give him the bad news of her death. Before she went to India she had had a long conversation with my father about going to India. He was telling her not to go to India. But she said, "No, I have to go to India."

It is said some relationships are from a previous life and they complete unfinished business in this life. I feel such was the case between these two, Amrit and Amrit. They had a wonderful relationship of father and daughter. And for the time she contributed to my father's well being. My family and I will always be grateful to her. We prayed may God bless her soul in peace. For me she will always remain an angel.

OUT OF THE HOSPITAL AND INTO REHAB

After few days her infection cleared, and she was in stable condition, doctors at Lenox Hill Hospital said there was nothing more they can do medically. A social worker began to talk to me about finding a rehab place, which has the expertise to manage a patient with ventilator. The social worker gave us a list of places in Queens and Manhattan. We were to choose two or three places so that the social worker can submit the discharge report of my mother to these places. Hopefully one of the places will accept her.

I had no knowledge of any of the places. I had never visited any of them before. Now I had to search for a place to see what kind of facility they provide, how is their physical therapy program, how is the place itself. Is the place hygienic and clean? Are the people working there caring?

Some of these places can be far away and inconvenient for the family to visit every day. But I felt the place should be chosen based on what will be good for the patient and not the family. If one can have both, that's the best.

I visited five rehabilitation centers, one in Manhattan and four in Queens. It was a depressing day. I cried very loud. I felt very helpless and angry at the circumstances. I saw many patients on ventilators in these places. It seems some patients are just waiting to die. Some of them probably pray for death to come so they can be free from the pain and helplessness. What kind of a quality of life do they have lying in beds, breathing with machines, being fed by tubes, unable to speak? My inner thoughts were, 'Would I like to live this kind of life?" The answer came from inside: "No I would chose not to live if I was given the choice."

But death is not in our hands. I wondered what was my mother really feeling. Does she think sometimes that she wishes she were not living anymore? As I know her, she believes in accepting life as God gives it to you. This is her strength. I think it's hard to accept life on philosophical ideas sometimes, but when we feel helpless it gives us the strength to accept and be in that moment.

I liked the rehab center in Manhattan and the one in Flushing Queens. We had a new doctor for Mother. Her name is Dr. Noori. She practices in Queens and she is affiliated with the Flushing rehab center. She suggested we should take Mother to that center. Dr. Noori is certified in Internal Medicine, Pulmonary and Critical Care. Dr. Noori felt that she could help my mother get off the ventilator. So, we moved our mother to the Flushing rehab center on March 10 th 2004.

On March 10th 2004, hope: From Lenox Hill Hospital, my mother was moved to a rehab center in Queens, New York where patients are on ventilators. One hopes that at the rehab center, patients will get off the ventilator. A few days ago when I came here looking for a place for my mother, I met a woman, who was also on ventilator.

Today she was leaving the hospital. I brought her to meet my mother. I explained to my mother that a month ago the woman also was on a ventilator just like my mother and now she is going home without one. I told my mother there is a hope that she would be able to do that also. Looking at that woman I also had hope for my mother. Unfortunately, my mother was not able to come off the ventilator. She never came back home.

After being at the Flushing rehab center for a few days, my mother experienced internal bleeding with her Hematoma for a second time. Because of this complication, she was transferred to the North Shore Hospital in Forest Hills, Queens on March 15th 2004, under the care of Dr. Noori. Once again mother is in the hospital. The unpredictable hospital journey begins again.

BACK TO THE HOSPITAL

At the North Shore Hospital, some days Mother was okay. Some days she was not okay. Some days she has one infection and then it gets cured. A few days later a different kind of infection… and then it is cured. It is a very normal occurrence in the hospital.

It seemed Mother had become resigned to her body - let it happen, do whatever you want to her body. It's understandable. Anyone will feel that way after going through so many procedures. We were going to the hospital everyday to the point where it became a familiar activity. It also became the best moment of my day to see her, touch her, massage her face, forehead and feet. She would also give me her blessings. She would put her hand on my head, a gesture too strong for words. I wish instead of the hospital I could see her at the restaurant or at home as before.

At the hospital, they always have English language program on the TV. I brought a TV with video player for my mother. I wanted to bring Indian language programs for her. I recorded programs from Indian television every night. In the morning I played the tape fast forward and took out scenes of death, hospitals or people dying. I re-recorded some dancing songs over those portions. I did not want her to see such scenes and get depressed. I got her many comedy movies. I tried to find Indian movies that did not have violence and people dying. Sometimes it was hard to find Indian movies that did not have those kinds of scenes. Here I was trying to protect her from not seeing scenes of death, but she probably thought of her own death coming any day. Right or wrong, it was just my way to safe guard her thinking. It may have been naive or foolish of me.

After the Hematoma got taken care, the goal now was to get her off the ventilator. In order to do that she needs to be watched 24-hours a day, so that anytime her oxygen level is low, it can be adjusted. A nurse watches more than seven patients in a shift so it is not possible for nurse to watch constantly any patient.

We visited our mother everyday and spent few hours with her. But we hired two private companion nurses to watch over Mother in 12-hour shifts each every day. Their work was to stay with her in her room. They can inform at nursing station in case of low oxygen, so that it can be taken care of. These companion nurses could also do other things for my mother such as comb her hair, put on cream lotion, play music for her, change video tapes and to give her company when we are not there. These nurses liked my mother. They said she reminded them of their own mother. She is very loving. It was a good thing my brother and I did for our mother. It made us feel more comfortable to know these companion nurses were there.

My sister Neeru came again from India to visit Mother. This time her husband R. P. also came with her for a few days. My mother was very happy to see Mr. R.P. He knew she loved him and he also loved my mother - his mother-in-law. And why not? He has her heart, her daughter. My sister is a wonderful lady and she had made her contributions to R.P.'s life. R.P admits that. If my sister is wonderful, my mother has something to do with it, some contribution.

When the time came for R.P to leave New York, I gave my mother some money to give to R.P. It was for an Indian tradition: when a son-in-law comes to visit his in-laws, they give him money along with some gifts (the amount is irrelevant.) The gift can be sweets and some cloth (or a shirt, pants). It is a symbolic way to wish the person prosperity. At the time my mother was not able to talk. I did not want her to feel helpless to do this ritual. I knew it would make her happy to give back to R.P and it did. It was the last time she ever saw R. P. When my brothers came to know about this, they said that it was a very caring thing to do.

With care, love, and encouragement, again my mother began her journey to get off the ventilator, little improvements day by day.

Memories from the North Shore hospital:

MARCH 15TH 2004- MY FATHER KISSED MY MOTHER ON THE LIPS

One day while Mother was at North Shore Hospital in Forest Hills, Queens, my father and I were in her room. Just as we were leaving my father felt so much love for my mother, he kissed her on lips. My mother blushed. It was the first time ever I saw my father kissing my mother on the lips; perhaps he thought this would be his last kiss? It was very nice for me to witness that exchange of love between them. Traditionally speaking in the Indian culture it's rare for a son to see that.

MOTHERS DAY LETTER FROM 1995

One day, I found a letter in my parents' apartment that I wrote to my mother on Mother's Day in the year 1995. I read the letter to my mother. She smiled. It was a long letter telling her how much I love her, and what a great mother she is. Then I told her, I love her much more now. It has grown in years. And she smiled again.

NURSING HOME

After spending some time at the North shore hospital my mother had gotten off the ventilator. On May 5th 2004, Mother was moved to Isabella Nursing Home in upper Manhattan.

In the summer of 2004 when my mother was in stable condition at Isabella, I was offered a very good role as a villain in an Indian movie to be shot in New York and nearby areas for four weeks. I explained to my mother about the role and asked what I should do. She said to me "Do it."

"Do you know what it means if I do the role?" I explained, "I will not be able to come to see you everyday. You will have to take care of yourself." She nodded yes.

I did the role. After the shooting was over, I brought her the album of the photos of the shoot with my pictures. She looked at all the photographs three times and touched my face in every photo. She gave me thumps up after looking though the photos. In this film, I get killed and I am lying on the floor in blood. I did not put those pictures in the album. I did not want her to see pictures of me like that even if they were fake.

MOTHER'S DAY, MAY 2004

On this Mother's Day, everybody was present. All her four children and many others who have adopted my mother as a surrogate mother came to celebrate. We all brought her gifts and flowers. Everyone spoke and gave her Mother's day greetings.

We read poems to her, explaining how much we all loved her, and what a great mother she had been. Father got very emotional and spoke, reviewing her life as a mother. He was so emotional that at the end of the speech, it made all of us very emotional. I guess in the back of our mind, we were afraid this might be the last Mother's Day that we would get to celebrate with her.

And it was.

AMRIT SAYS GOODBYE TO TARA

July 18th 2004 Sunday: For the last few months I have been taking my father to sat sang (spiritual congregation/meetings) in New Jersey. It gives him happiness and peace. Today as on other Sundays, after the sat sang we went to visit Mother in the rehab nursing home in the afternoon.

When we walked in the room, Mother was sitting in the chair. I touched her feet, and said hello; she touched my head. I went to sit near the window looking out the city from 9th floor. I sat near the window so that my father can have his own time with my mother.

I turn slightly around and saw my father holding the right hand of my mother. They were looking at each other, and some communication was going on between them. My mother with her left hand took my father's and put it on her stomach. She kept looking at him right into his eyes. She looked very emotional, conveying to him that she was very tired now and she cannot live any more like this and that she wanted to go.

My father held both of her hands, smiled and whispered some words to her, which I could not hear. Then I saw her smile back at him as if they had made some pact. They kept looking at each other. I told my mother that many people were inquiring about her at the sat sang. I massaged her feet and legs as I did every time I saw her. After some time my Father and I left. Before leaving, he touched her face and forehead and then kissed her forehead. I saluted her and she saluted me back as always.

On the next day, my father got weaker and did not feel well. In the coming days he became more frail, weaker and quieter. He felt too weak to visit my mother for many days, even when I asked him to come with me. He said physically he was not able to come. He was too weak to sat sang also, so we did not go for next two Sundays.

"It is very hard for me to see your mother like this," he explained to me one day. "I feel more in pain after seeing her although I understand this is the reality of her condition." Then he added further, "Your mother understands my not going to see her very often. She knows how I feel."

July 18th 2004 was the last time he physically saw my mother. Many days later on August 4th 2004, he told me that when he saw my mother on July 18th, he told her Good-bye. She told him she wanted to go and he said to her, "You go and I will follow you."

MY LAST DAY WITH MOTHER

On August 1st 2004, a Sunday, I had wanted to spend all day with my mother. It was very nice weather outside. My father was not feeling well, and he was not eating. We did not go to sat sang that day. I took some food for my father. I spent part of the day with him. Then I went to see my mother. I was well dressed, because later in the evening I was going to the birthday party of the granddaughter of Mr. Kalaish Sharma and Mr. Sunil Dutt. As I walked in, my mother was sitting in a chair looking very beautiful and I said to her, "Bibi, you are looking very beautiful today. I like having a beautiful mother."

Since she was not able to speak, she gestured with her hand to say, 'you are looking very handsome too - where are you going?' I told her I was going to a birthday party because she had given the blessing three weeks earlier on the phone to Mr. Sharma who happened to call while I was sitting with my mother that day. He asked her blessings on the phone. I reminded her that she had dinner once with Mr. Sunil Dutt at the Ayurveda Café. She remembered. After some time she wanted to lie in the bed. So she did. I was sitting very close to her.

She made a gesture for me to come closer to her. She pulled my hair and gave me a kiss on my cheeks. Then she touched my whole face. When she came to my jaw she started pressing my cheeks to force a smile. Her left hand went all over my face and then on my shoulders and then all the way to my hand. At this point, I felt melted inside. A feeling of unconditional love cannot be explained in words alone. It's magic when you feel the touch of total unconditional love. I will never forget it. Even today when I close my eyes and I think of that experience it gives chills in my whole body and fills me with incredible love. I feel so blessed.

By some cosmic intervention I asked my mother, "Are you okay in your heart and mind?" She waved her head signaling yes.

"Are you at peace with yourself are you accepting what God has done?" I asked. She nodded her head saying yes. I asked, "Are you 100% sure?" She nodded again yes. And she smiled. I held her hand throughout the time I sat there with her, then it was time for me to leave. As I got up, I stood near her feet. She looked at me. There was a song playing on the radio, an Indian song about a mother's love for her children. She pointed to me to hear that song.

"Are you telling me you love me this much?" I asked. She nodded her head saying yes. I opened both my arms to the fullest length saying, "I love you this much and more." I threw a flying kiss towards her and I said, "This is on your left cheek." She smiled. I made a salute signal with my right hand saying good-bye to her. She made a salute to me with her left hand and she smiled. Then I left for the party. That was the last time I saw her.

AUGUST 2ND 2004, MONDAY

The next day, a Monday, my father was not feeling well. I took him to three different doctors for various tests in Queens. I ended up spending the whole day with him in doctors' offices. In the evening around 8:30 PM, we came over Tri-borough Bridge and I said to my father "Let's go see my mother." He said, No, he was not feeling well and was very tired. So I dropped him at his home and by that time it was almost 10 PM. I could not go to see my mother that day. During the day my brother had visited her with his whole family.

I went to Ayurveda Café and told many things about my mother to the employees. I told them she was the reason we opened Ayurveda Café. She lit the first fire in the kitchen when we opened the Café. I picked up my food, and was going home. I got a call on my cell phone from my mother's companion nurse (we had two private companion nurses for last months to be with my mother for 24 hours, 12 hours each shift.) I noticed the number on my cell. It was not the landline number from my mother's room. I asked the nurse why she was calling from cell phone. She said the land line phone was not working today.

Every night, I would say good night to my mother. The nurse would put the phone on Mother's ear and I would speak about my day, tell her I love her and say goodnight. Then my mother would make a gesture suggesting the conversation was over and the nurse would close the phone.

That evening, the nurse put the cell phone on my mother's ear; I said to her that I was sorry I could not come that day. I was busy taking care some things, and then the cell phone got disconnected. The nurse redialed the number and told me my mother did not make the gesture that conversation was over. The nurse said, "Here talk to her." She put the cell phone back on my mother's ear.

"I'm okay," I started telling my mother. "I just picked up the food from your restaurant - Ayurveda Café. I am going home. I will take a shower, then I will have my dinner. I was just talking about you with the employees at Ayurveda Café. I will see you tomorrow. I love you. Goodnight. You also take rest, sleep well."

Then the Nurse came on the phone and said my mother made the gesture the conversation is over. I told the nurse, "Good-night. Thank you, for taking care of my mother. See you tomorrow." I reached my home, took shower and had my dinner.

It was around 11:00 PM when I got a call from the nursing home that my mother was not breathing, they did CPR and she was not responding.

For a few seconds I did not know what to say - then it occurred to me what happened. On August 2nd Monday at 11:30 PM, my mother had passed away in the rehab nursing home. I told the nurse I am coming. I called my brother Chander and told him. I called my sister in India. I called my elder brother Ram Raj in Canada.

I met Chander outside the garage. I said I cannot drive and you will have to drive. Chander and I went to the nursing home and walked into her room.

She was lying in bed.

All IV's and machines were off.

She was looking very calm and beautiful.

She had the divine peace on her face.

It looked as if she had just gone to sleep.

I sat down and talked to her as we used to do.

I held her hand and broke out in tears.

I started to cry out loud.

Chander was also crying.

Chander and I, we both held each other, and cried.

Then I wanted some time alone with her.

I kept looking at her.

I put my head in her lap, cried. I let it all out.

I was talking to her as if she were still alive and could hear me.

I know she could hear me.

I told her I loved her very much, I will miss her.

Chander was also shocked and wept. He also had some time alone with her in the room.

I called my sister and my elder brother while I was in the room to confirm what has happened.

After some time we left because they cannot keep the body too long in the room. They have to prepare the body to put in the morgue.

We did not go to our father to inform because he has not being feeling well and we did not want to give the news in the night.

That night when I got home, I felt a part of me had been lost. My body went into a state of shock. I felt numb.

NUMBNESS

Last night I could not sleep and then at some point, my body gave up and dozed off as I was feeling very numb. Woke up this morning and planned to go to my father's home with my brother to tell him.

How will he feel? On August 3rd, in the morning, after being with him for some time, we told my father, "Baoji kal raat bibi chali gaye" (Father, Mother passed away last night.)

He said, "Mannu patha hai" (I know.) It seemed as if he really knew. Then he added, "It's good she passed away. Now she is free and she is with God.

I don't know how he knew, but then again when you have loved each other for 60 years, there must be some heart connections between two people, which can be felt in a silent and distant space of the universe. I guess when the hearts and consciousness of two people are connected; they can feel beyond space and communication. One heart will know what is happening to other.

I wondered about all this time when we were not telling Mother that Father was not feeling well, in order to protect her. But she might have known. I asked my father if would he like to go to see her body. First he said no, then some time later he said yes. But then we felt it may not be a good idea for him to see her body in a morgue. I discussed this with him and he agreed. Not only would it have been very difficult for him – it would also be difficult for me to see my mother's body in morgue. I have never seen a body in a morgue but I can imagine it must feel very strange to see someone you love, their body laying in a morgue, in a refrigerator.

I spent most of the day with my father talking about Mother. It seemed he was prepared to face this. He has been expecting it. But he still seemed a little lost and quieter that day.

We started to call people to inform them. We made the arrangement for my mother's funeral to be held on Saturday, August 7th at 11:30 AM at the Gerard J. Neufeld Funeral Home in Queens. My sister Niru was coming from India, my elder brother Ram Raj and his family was coming from Canada.

All the people we informed they were very sad to know. They loved my mother. I could feel people's genuine affection and respect for my mother. Many of them told me stories about their beautiful interactions with my mother.

In the days to come I cannot recollect what exactly I was feeling. But I do know I felt very numb and lost.

Premiere of "Lonely in America"

Amrit and Tara, proud parents

Amrit and Tara, in love

Below: Amrit and Tara, at the beginning of their

Tara and Amrit 60 years together

Tara with a beautiful smile

Tara at the hospital

Tara and Amrit traveling across Europe

Tara with son Chander and her grandson

Tara and Amrit with sons, Tirlok and Chander

Amrit putting the ring on at their 50th anniversary

Amrit with the Chander family

Amrit with his grandmother

Amrit with grandmother,
mother, father, and
siblings

Tara and Amrit, always full of joy

Tara_and_Amrit,_new_years_party

Amrit and Tara with RP

Amrit and Tara, never too old to have fun

Tirlok and Amrit, taken 2 days before his death

THE FUNERAL DAY

All of our family members reached the funeral home. Her body was all dressed up with makeup, lying in a coffin box with flowers. She was looking very peaceful and beautiful.

Before I helped my father sit down near her, he put a red color chunni (an Indian shawl) around her neck, covering her head. It's a symbol for a married woman in Indian culture. When a woman gets married she also wears red during the wedding. My mother looked like a bride in that red shawl.

I put a shawl on her, saying you may feel cold on the way. I was talking to her as if she could hear me. I was looking at her body; sitting near her, touching her forehead. I wanted her to know what I was feeling at that moment, before her body was cremated. It may sound strange but it was nice to spend time with my mother one last time. It was my last chance to see her in physical form and touch her.

My father sat next to her the whole time, looking at her. He touched her few times. I saw tears in his eyes. When he first saw her that day, he just kept looking at her. I wondered what he might have thought when saw her first. I was feeling so much compassion for him. I cannot imagine what it must feel to lose your companion, your life partner, your love after being together for sixty years. Even though it is the ultimate reality of life. One has no choice but to accept it.

There were over 300 people at the funeral. The place was filled to the maximum. Ninety five percent of the people were there because they really wanted to be there. They were not there for the social norm reasons. Spiritual songs were sung. Speeches were given about life and death. The music that played was very calm. Many people spoke of their feelings.

My brother Chander spoke very beautifully. He said when he used to see his mother giving so much love to everyone, he would wonder, will she have left any love for him? Then he realized that she has so much love to give, it was in abundance. I agreed with him.

My brother's wife Karen spoke about her first meeting with my mother. She said that she and Chander had been dating for a while. When it came to the question of marriage, Chander said, "We will have to go to India and meet my mother." Karen wondered what his mother would say. When they reached India and Karen first met my mother, she saw how my mother looked at Chander with so much love. She knew my mother would accept her.

Many people spoke about the wonderful encounters they had with my mother. The funeral was a very loving good-bye to a woman who was full of love, not only as a mother, but in all her relationships. She was a remarkable woman.

Everybody saw her for the last time. Then she was taken in a funeral procession to Fresh Pond Crematory. At the crematory my elder brother Ram Raj pressed the button to light the flames for cremation. My sister Niru, who was standing next to me watching this, broke down. She started to cry and said, "Bibi Gayee" (Mother is gone.) I was crying myself, but tried to console her. Many people let go and were crying out loud. I looked at my father who was in silence.

HUMAN ERROR VS DESTINY

In the days that followed my mother's funeral I wrestled with the question, did she die because of human error or was it her destiny?

Sometimes things go wrong in hospitals. No one does it intentionally. But it can happen because someone was not being responsible in their Job. Someone was not paying attention when they should have been while doing their job. Someone made a decision without complete knowledge; someone made a mistake somewhere along the way.

When a mistake happens, it can cause pain, and more harm to the patient who may feel worse. Sometimes mistakes cannot be cured. Those mistakes are fatal and they lead to lot of physical and emotional pain for the patient and their loved ones. How to handle that? How to come to terms to accept that fatal mistake? I have been facing this dilemma. Things were done in irresponsible manner to my mother and that changed of her from almost ready to come home to never will come home.

That mistake set the chain reaction to no return. On December 26th 2003, a social worker was discussing with me plans to take my mother home. On December 29th, 2003 my mother was on Comoden and a nurse ruptured blood vessels in her stomach while injecting. The nurse injected at the wrong angle. My mother complained about the pain, but she was not given medical attention and treatment for more than 10 hours. It caused a chain reaction that led to many complications.

After this fatal mistake my mother never turned around. She suffered for seven months, never came home and died in rehab on August 2, 2003. And a year later my father died because he did not want to live without her.

Later two outside doctors told me that the hospital staff at Lenox Hill made the mistake. I could hold them responsible in court and sue them. I do have enough evidence.

It is one of the most haunting thoughts that I have been living with. It's a conflict I have no answer for. I have to make a choice and try to live with it. Each one has its own consequences.

Did she suffer and die…

…Because of Human Error!

…Or was it her destiny?

No Matter which reason I choose to believe, my mother will not come back to life.

But the choice of my belief will have effect on me,

On my emotional well-being, and on my life.

My mother, no matter what, would not have been happy knowing that after she was gone I would be miserable. So I made the decision to accept within myself that it was her destiny to go.

MY FIRST BIRTHDAY WITHOUT MOTHER

October 18ᵗʰ 2004: Today is my birthday. In the morning when I woke up, I missed the phone call of my mother. The first call always used to be hers.

And she will say, "Good morning Bacche (my child), Happy Birthday." She will try to sing. I would have lunch with her on my birthday. She would distribute sweets on the following Sunday in the sat sang. She would give money and sweets to workers at our restaurant and some other friends she had. She would proudly say, "Today is Tirlok's Birthday." She would give five dollars to each employee. She always enjoyed doing that. She did this on the birthdays of my brothers and sister as well.

It was the first birthday I've had without my mother; I missed her very much. I cried a few times and then I consoled myself by saying that she is with me in the spiritual form. I began to feel her with me. I then spent the day with my father.

"Happy Birthday," he said.

"Thank you, Father, for bringing me to this world," I said.

"Thank you, son. You are a gift from God. I am lucky to have you," he replied.

My father talked to me about the importance of feeling love in personal relationships. I ate dinner at our restaurant, sitting at the same table where my mother used to sit. I decided to give out some money to all our employees in restaurant; "I'm giving this on behalf of my mother."

THANKSGIVING

I am getting ready to go to my brother Chander's house for the Thanksgiving celebration. This will be the first one without our mother. The loss of a loved one hurts more on special days but at the same time the grief you feel gives more depth.

The absence of my mother awakened many memories I had with her on this special holiday over the years. I remembered spending the Thanksgiving of November 2003 with her. I would have never imagined this would be the last Thanksgiving I would be spending with her. The images of last year are very clear in my mind. But now I can acknowledge to myself that she is not here anymore. I did not want to color the celebration with pain, instead choosing to feel her presence in a positive way.

My brother has always been a great host as he was this time. My father joined us in the celebration. We all acknowledged that mother was not there that day. We all remembered her love. I needed to process associated feelings and memories of the absence of my mother. I asked my father to recite one of the poems he had written about life. The meaning of the poem is:

> The child is born, the child is raised…
>
> …the child becomes an adult, gets married, has children, works, raises children…
>
> … the children get older, get married…
>
> … then the person gets old and leaves this world…
>
> … And if the person has lived a life with integrity, has contributed to the society, has done no harm to anybody, then the life is completed.

That day I gave my father two beautiful silk shirts. He was very happy with my gesture of giving him the gift.

That was the last Thanksgiving my father spent with us.

BACK TO WORK

At all my events, such as film shoots or a premiere of a movie, my parents were my special guests. I would invite them on the stage to the premieres of my movies, introduce them, thank them and seek their blessings for continued success. They always felt very proud to witness my event. After my mother's death, as life has to move on, I started to work again. Father was okay and was living at home, having a 24-hour nurse. The nurse was very good she liked my father and my father was comfortable.

Before my mother went to the hospital I was working on launching a platform to promote Indian American artists in film and television. So I picked up on the idea again and decided to do the first NRI TV film awards, in the model of the Academy Awards. The NRI Award show was to honor and recognize, from an historical perspective, Independent Indian-American films made in America between 1960 and 2004. It was to be a pioneering and historical event for Indian-American cinema.

I explained to my father what I was planning to do and received his blessings. I told him the date was December 5th 2004. The planning of the award show was going very well. The 'Who's Who' of the Indian-American community in New York had already confirmed they would attend the event. On November 29th 2004 my father went into the hospital again. I was hoping he would be out of the hospital by December 4th to attend my event on the 5th.

On December 3rd I was informed by the hospital that he would have to stay there much longer. Although he was looking forward to attending my event, he said, "It's not in my luck to see your event, but I am sure it will go well. You have my blessings".

On December 5th, on the day of event, I went to see him in the morning. "I will miss you at the event," I said.

He replied, "I will be there - I will be there." I touched his feet and embraced him tight. He also embraced me tightly and gave me a long kiss on my cheek.

The event was a great success and it was later aired all over USA twice on TV Asia. I carried in my pocket a ball made of multi-layered cloth. (We used this ball with my mother to do her physical exercise for arms. She used to throw the ball at us, we would throw it back at the bed near her hand and she would throw back again.) It had the smell of her touch. It had her energy. This was my way of carrying her touch with me that day. In my speech at the event, I paid my tribute to my mother and mentioned that she was with God in the Heaven now.

Then I gave a tribute to all mothers and said my mother used to say all mothers are the same but all kids may not be the same. I also gave regards from my father to the audience. After the event, many people said to me they were touched by the tribute I gave to my mother. I wonder why as kids we want so badly for our parents to witness and know about our success?

HOSPITAL TO KATERI RESIDENCE

I often brought my father for checkups even while my mother was living. When it became clear that my mother was not coming home, my father began to slowly deteriorate from there on. There was nothing wrong with him medically but he was not feeling well. He seemed broken inside.

A few days after the death of my mother he became really unwell. He had to spend two months in the hospital on 113th and Amsterdam Avenue. My brother and me visited him everyday. We brought him Indian food and sat with him. He had a television and I brought many VHS tapes of spiritual programs for him to watch.

From the hospital on 113th my father was sent to the Kateri nursing and rehabilitation center on 87th and Riverside drive. I remember asking my father if he would rather be home, and he said, "No if I go home all I will think about is your mother, everything will remind me of her and our time together. I would rather live in the Kateri Nursing home. Here I can see people everyday, I get to talk to them and keep my mind busy also I am taken care of better here."

My brother and I went to visit him at Kateri everyday. We would bring him food from the restaurant and at some point in the day either my brother or I would sit with him while he ate (we would both go separately so my father had more company). In the Kateri nursing home there was a large upscale meeting area on the penthouse floor. It was glass enclosed and very pleasant to sit down there. It did not look like a rehab center.

I would purposely arrange meetings with my friends and business associates to meet in the Kateri residence meeting area. This way my father could join in our meetings as well. I did this so his routine would change everyday at the Kateri residence. Many of the people who met my father would walk away much happier and sometimes wiser after having met with my father.

One day after I had brought him some lunch, he got angry with me for something. I said nothing and we parted. Later he called me on the phone and said, "I'm sorry I got mad with you." I said, "It's okay, you are the father, you're allowed to be angry with me." I went back to Kateri later that evening with some ice cream. My father was surprised, "Oh, you came back?" I said "yes I brought some ice cream with me, so we can have it together." He was very happy to see me. It was important for me to see him that day so he wouldn't continue to regret his outburst from before.

That night my father and I spoke until midnight. I knew my father wasn't on speaking terms with his brother at that time. I asked him, "Would you like to speak to uncle?" My father said, "Yes." I dialed my uncle's number on my phone and handed it to my father. They talked for a long time, the call ending with both of them in tears. As a son, I felt I should help my father to complete all of his relationships before he dies. It is necessary to have no regrets when you are at the end of your life. Sometimes relationships require asking for forgivingness, sometimes they require forgiving.

During the beginning of my father's time at Kateri he didn't speak about mother. We spent that first mother's day with my father at the Kateri residence. At the end the day he said to me "Your mother was an angel. She followed through with her commitment to me and she was very nice to me." after that day my father began to talk openly about her again. I enjoyed listening to him.

He told me one day, "your mother and I talked about death when she was healthy. I told her we did not come to this world together, and we won't leave together. But we must be thankful to God for the time he has given us together."

My brother Chander gave him a high quality pair of sunglasses and at times my father would put on the glasses and sit by the windowsill looking at the skyline of New Jersey, and the boats in the Hudson River. This must have been his time to reflect on his inner side. He also enjoyed going to satang with me every Sunday.

I tried to make his time at the Kateri residence as comfortable and colorful as I could.

During that time I had done a commercial for PBS. The day they informed me the first time the commercial would be airing I was with my father at Kateri. I took my father into the dining room, which had a TV. The room was full of other residents. Upon seeing the commercial many of them said "Mr. Malik look! Your son is on television!" He smiled and was very proud.

The last father's day we spent with my father was at the Kateri center.

THE DAY POPE DIED

I had been grieving about the death of my mother. I was also faced with my father being in the hospital and my knowing what is coming. It's just a matter of time. During this time, everyone knows the Pope was not feeling well and eventually died.

My internal thoughts were: here is an important figure

He has the world's best doctors to take care of him 24 hours a day,

He has the best of medical facilities available to him,

He has billions of people praying for him,

He probably has done no harm to anybody and has the good Karma,

Then, when the time came, he died.

It reminded me that no matter who you are, death comes to everyone sooner or later. But still, it brings sadness for the loved ones who are left behind. For some reason, this was intellectually comforting to me at the time.

A DRIVE WITH MY FATHER

This was the last day I spent with my father. It feels like a dream. It seems to me my father and God wanted to make sure I would be given the last sign of love from my father in physical form in such abundance that it would last me forever. I felt my mother and God were riding with me in the car that Sunday. My mother always used to say I was her innocent boy with a gentle and loving heart. My parents were always worried about me. But somehow they also knew ultimately it is the genuineness, truthfulness of a loving heart that brings you happiness. And that happiness does not mean it will not bring you sadness, but that the happiness would be deep rooted and in its purest form.

That Sunday morning, my father and I were driving to a sat sang in New Jersey. On the way, I connected the phone to my sister in New Delhi and handed the phone to my father (I always did that so that he could speak to her.) My father said to my sister, "It feels good to hear your voice. My heart likes it." He had a long conversation with her about the well- being of her, her family and her husband Mr. R. P. He told her he loves her, may God always bless her and he spoke about some other things in general. Then he also spoke to her husband Mr. R. P. at length.

After disconnecting the phone he said to me R. P. is a good man. He told me that he felt good that his daughter was married to a good man, that he made the right choice of choosing Mr. R. P. as my sister's husband. What I felt listening to him was that as a father he was happy about his daughter. That's the wish of every father.

I turned on the tape player in the car, a gazal (song) by Jagjit Singh. The meaning of the song was, "I am wondering on the roads after leaving my home and there is no one to call me back." Looking back I feel it's ironic for him to be listening to that song that day. At the sat sang he said hello to everyone. We ate lunch together while sitting on the floor. For the last several times, he ate lunch while sitting in a wheel chair with table in front of him. I asked him, "Do you want to sit in the wheel chair?" He simply replied, "That's not needed."

A lady member of the sat sang recently had a grandson. My parents knew her very well. When she told my father about the grandson, he said to her "Bring him here." My father then asked me to give him some money. She brought in her grandson and my father gave him the money and blessed him. In Indian culture giving money is a symbolic blessing for prosperity, however the amount of money given is of no importance.

We were among the last people who left sat sang. My father had a conversation with almost everybody there. On the way back to New York, I started to play music but then I shut it off and said to my father, "Let's talk and say something." We talked the whole ride back to New York. It was a one-hour ride. We spoke of many things. He said to me "Tirlok bête (Tirlok, son) you are something. May God always bless your happiness. You are always ready to give, may God always keep you that way. Always keep spirituality a part of your life along with the worldly success. Always go towards salvation." He spoke very highly about my brother Chander. He said he was lucky God had given him such a good wife and children. He told me at his birth time, his parents were informed by the astrologer that he would be lucky with family.

I asked him what is the most important thing he remembered about his Father (my grandfather.) He said, "He was a man of integrity. In his heart he was very pure." I asked about his mother (my grandmother.) He said, "She was very loving and very spiritual." I asked my father to recite a poem written by him. He did and the meaning of the poem is "Amrit, whether you agree or do not agree, whatever is supposed to happen will happen. So it is better to agree, because that is the way God wants".

At that point I asked him point blank, "Have you agreed with life - whatever has happened?" He answered, "Yes, I've had a wonderful life." On the rest of the way, he told me many wonderful stories and spoke about lessons of life. I told him later in the evening I was getting an award that evening for my contribution as an Indian American film maker by an association in Long Island New York. He was happy to know that. And I promise this is true: as we approached the tunnel into Manhattan, we saw a rare sight: a double rainbow in the sky.

In the early evening, I left him at the rehab nursing home (where he was staying). As always, I touched his feet and said I love you. He touched my head and said, "Me too" (I love you too.) I saw him wheeling his chair to his room. I took the elevator back to the ground floor. That evening I went to Long Island (New York.) On the way back I was very happy and thinking about the whole day. What a wonderful day it was that I spent with my father.

AUGUST 29TH, ANOTHER SAD MONDAY

August 29th, Monday morning around 9:00 A.M., I got a call from the nursing home informing me, "Mr. Malik is not breathing." It took me few seconds to understand. The nurse said he did not come for breakfast so they went to his room. I said we would be coming soon. Keep him in his room. I called Chander, Bansal, my sister and some other people. I called my elder brother Ram Raj in Canada. He was supposed to come to New York on August 28th (yesterday), but he postponed his plan. I felt compassion for him thinking what he might be feeling. I, Chander and Bansal went to the nursing home, saw father in his room; he was looking peaceful and divine. Amrit had crossed over to the other world while sleeping.

The nurses and hospital staff at the rehab center all felt sad knowing my father had passed. They liked him very much. They said he was always smiling and saying hello to everybody. One nurse told me that last week when he was sitting in the dining room among other residents, he was telling them, "We shall never be afraid of death. It's a reality of life, and we are all going to die one day. So be happy, be thankful to God, and enjoy today." At that moment it became apparent that all the conversations, and interactions he had with me, Chander, Karen, Neeru, Bansal, the staff at the rehab, people at sat sang and many others in the last 2 weeks indicated that he knew where he was going and he was at total peace and ready to go. He felt his work on this Earth was done and he chose to go.

Looking back at the last day I spent with him, I am convinced that he knew in some way he was going to go. All my conversations from the day before felt like a cosmic intervention. As a son I feel blessed to have had that day. It reminded me of the day I spent with my mother just before she passed away. My brother Chander told me he also had many loving conversations with Father, in recent times, indicating that my father was looking for closure before his departure. My brother's wife Karen told me that my father told her a week before, "I have been talking to your Bibiji (mother)." It reminds me of the conversation he had with my mother on July18th 2004, "You go and I will follow you." Today he did it.

They both passed away in the month of August. They both passed away on a Monday.

In the coming days we began preparations one more time to say good-bye to our parent. My sister said she was not coming; she cannot handle the image of cremating the body. She has not been able to forget the image of mother's cremation. She wanted to keep the memory of her conversation she had father as her last moment with him.

Amrit Malik, the Doctor

My father, when he was a young man, met a homeopathic doctor named Daya Shanker, in Delhi. Dr. Shanker suggested that my father study homeopathy. He felt my father would understand it and would do something good for people. My father did and decided to practice for free. For fifty years he did this. He never charged anyone.

I've seen him giving medicines to people and people coming back and touching his feet with gratefulness and regards. He did that in New York also. Even as children, he would give us homeopathic medicine any time anything happened. As children, we made fun of my father sometimes, calling it lolopathy ("lolo" meaning silly, stupid.) As kids we thought modern medicine was the cure for everything. We did not understand until we grew up.

As I got older I began to appreciate and understand why my father did not give us the modern medicine when we had small childhood ailments. He was also aware that sometimes modern medicine was necessary when homeopathy could not help. I still have with me his sixty-year old wooden box in which he kept bottles of homeopathic medicine.

Amrit Malik, My father, My Therapist

Over the years in my life, many times I was disturbed, angry and lost. Some of those moments I shared with my father. He would listen, console, and suggest to me, "Don't keep dead snakes around your neck son. Let them go. The people who hurt you, or betray you – forgive them and move on." As a young man, sometimes I thought that my father has not lived in America, what could he possibly know about America? But then I realized my father has lived a full life and has wisdom to give; the kind of wisdom that can transcend culture. So I listened to him and dropped the dead snakes from around my neck. My life has had ups and downs. There have been wonderful moments and there have been betrayals.

Another piece of advice my father gave me: "keep your needs minimum, and you will always be happy. But if god gives you a buffet, go for it."

He also said to "keep your spiritual side always intact. This will bring you peace."

The lessons I learned from my father continue to be therapy sessions for me, even after he is gone. Whenever I am faced with a dilemma, I remember what my father told me and use his guidance. I have seen my father consoling and giving advice to many other people in distress over the years.

FATHER'S FUNERAL

It's the same funeral home, same crematory, where mother's funeral was done in August 2004. I even requested the same exact location of the crematorium where my mother was cremated. Again, the funeral home was filled to its capacity with more than 300 people. There was the same spiritual music, many of the same people, some new ones, tributes by loved ones and friends. It was very much a loving good-bye to father as it was to mother.

I sat next to my father; spoke to him as if he were listening, whispered things to him, knowing after couple of hours I will never see his physical body again. I looked at his face, and remembered how last year he came walking into this place at the time of my mother's funeral, his wife's funeral, and today we are here for his funeral. Today he cannot walk.

Life changes and you never know. In the funeral tribute, Chander said Amrit was the kind of man who, when he did something for somebody, never waited to hear thank you. I agree with my brother Chander's words, "Amrit was the purest man I have ever known in my life." After paying tributes by many loved ones, we took his body in a procession to crematory. At the crematory, his body was placed at the same location where mother's body was cremated. My elder brother Ram Raj pressed the button to start flames for cremating the body. Many of us broke down, some with tears and some in silence. We came outside; it was a very sunny day.

We have just said good-bye to a yogi named Amrit Malik. I looked up and wondered, is he sitting with mother right now?

EULOGY FOR AMRIT

AMRIT MALIK (APRIL 7, 1926 - AUGUST 29, 2005)

Amrit Malik was born in 1926 in a small town in Punjab, Northern India. The astrologer informed his parents, Mr. Sant Ram and Bhagirithi Devi, at his birth that he will be lucky to the family. He was the oldest of four children - he had two brothers and a sister. After schooling Amrit was ready to start a family, so he got married (arranged) and then later on developed incredible love for his beautiful wife Tara. His journey as a young businessman took him to several towns in India and finally he settled in Delhi in the 1950s. After Amrit's brothers married, all the families lived in Delhi as a joint family and they worked together running a thread factory business. He was the father of three sons - Ram Raj, Tirlok, Chander and a daughter Neeru lovingly called "guddi."- (which means "doll".)

Sometime in the late 50's, he came to know about an alternative medicine system called homeopathy. He studied it in school and became a homeopathic doctor. He gave free medicine to hundreds of needy people throughout his life.

In 1952 he came across a spiritual congregation called "Nirankari Mission (Universal Brotherhood.)" The mission's philosophy is "whatever has been given to you, it's a gift from God for you to enjoy it, take care of it while you have it, but always remember it belongs to God." The mission also practiced "do not discriminate against people based on their color, religion, nationality or living habits. All are equal." He joined the mission, along with his family, and lived his life with the mission's principles - which were not about religion, but about spirituality. Amrit lived by these principles until the last day of his life.

In the early eighties Amrit and Tara lived with their oldest son Ram Raj, his wife Sunita, and their two children, Gaurav and Himani in Canada. Later in 1988 they came to live in New York City to be with their younger sons Tirlok and Chander. With their loving nature it was easy for them to make friends everywhere they went. Language and culture never came in their way because love is a universal language - that's the language Amrit and Tara always lived by. They visited the restaurants daily, co-owned by their sons and associates, on the West Side of Manhattan. They made many friends among the Indian and the Non-Indian community. Chander's family, his wife Karen, their children Levi and Skye always enjoyed their limitless love. Many people who came in contact with them, adopted them as surrogate parents. The list includes: Om & Sushil Bansal, Deva and Angie, Paul Gulati and his family, Ashok Wahi and family, and the restaurant staff and many others.

Amrit and Tara also had a very special relationship with their daughter "Guddi" and her husband Rajinder Singla and their children - Sonia, Sanjay, Raju, and their great-grandchildren who live in Delhi. They often spoke on the phone and visited them in India many times.

Amrit and Tara had their shares of ups and downs in marriage, as in any good relationship, but love was the binding force for both of them. Amrit once told his son Tirlok that "in love, you should never say to your partner you are mine, but rather say I am yours." Amrit said "when you say you are mine, that is possessiveness, but when you say I am yours that is surrender. And when you surrender to love, that is when magic happens." This is the magic Amrit had with his wife Tara, until the last day of his life.

Amrit was married to Tara for 60 years. At their 50th Wedding Anniversary they renewed their wedding vows in a ceremony among friends. Tara fell sick on December 18, 2003, for the first time ever, and was in the hospital/rehab until she passed away August 2, 2004. Watching her in the hospital had an effect on Amrit. But he never lost the faith in God and was aware of the blessings he had - knowing Tara for so many years and the children she gave him. His life was never the same after his beloved wife passed away. He spent his last few months in the hospital and rehab centers. During this time he reviewed his life and came to terms with it.

Sunday August 28, 2005 Tirlok took Amrit to Sat sung in New Jersey. In the satsang he gave his regards to everybody in a very special way. He felt healthy and happy. While in the car he told many wonderful stories and spoke about lessons of life. He blessed Tirlok with so much love and spoke about how he had such a wonderful family, children and life. While driving in the car, Tirlok asked his father to recite a poem written by Amrit that says "Amrit whether you agree or not agree whatever is supposed to happen, will happen so it is better to agree, because that is the way God wants." At this point Tirlok asked Amrit point blank "have you agreed with your life - whatever has happened?" Amrit answered, "Yes, I had a wonderful life."

On Monday morning when it was found that Amrit had crossed over to the other world while sleeping, it became apparent at that moment that in all the conversations and interactions he had with Chander, Karen, Tirlok, Neeru, Bansal, the staff at the rehab, people at Sat Sung and many others in the last two weeks, he knew where he was going and he was at total peace and ready to go. He felt his work on this Earth was done and he chose to go.

People who are left behind will love him forever and will miss him. We are so blessed to have known him. Everyone has their own way of saying things about him, but one common thought, which will be agreed by all, is a quote by Chander: "Amrit was the purest man I have ever known in my life."

Upon his birth, the astrologer was so right when he said: "this baby will be lucky to the family". YES. I am lucky to have him as my father and friend. (Tirlok Malik)

My family and I thank everyone for joining to say goodbye to a yogi named "Amrit Malik."

AFTERMATH

When you lose a parent, its effect is not like losing a relationship of one year, two years or even ten years, it's like losing a source of unconditional love. It's not possible to know what this feels like until you have experienced it for yourself.

I did not know how I would I feel after the funeral. Sometimes I felt a sense of liberation growing from the inner sight I had experienced over the last twenty-one months, watching my parents and then losing them. I feel with their blessings the road ahead will be beautiful.

I also felt a strong need to grieve for my parents, to come to terms with their death and then let go. I felt ultimately it would be a great liberation for me. It would make me more humble and compassionate. It would help me to grow as a person, and ultimately open more windows to my inner self. I feel the happy world is created when your inner self is at peace. I want to create my world to be happy; I want inner balance. It is said, 'Things will happen to you. Things will happen around you. But the most important is what happens inside you.'

With both of my parents gone, I asked myself about my role as a son, did I do right, did I do what I was supposed to do? I know one thing: whatever I did, I did from the heart and I did it with love. Yes I did, to the best of my capabilities. I could not stop them from leaving this world but I was able to make it loving and caring. I was able to assist them to create a passage to cross over into the other world. I feel yes, I was a good son to them. That is the satisfaction I have.

FAMILY SUPPORT AFTER FUNERAL

As I have said, I have two brothers and a sister. We each have a different nature in our personality and grieving process. It is natural in all human beings. I feel my brothers and sister are a reflection of my parents. After the parents are gone, I can see part of my parents in them, in spite of all our sibling conflicts.

Most siblings also have emotional perceptions about each other. One should not let these perceptions hinder the siblings from supporting one another. One should simply seek their support. There should be no judgment about this matter. All you need to do is support and check up on each other.

Parents are the link among siblings. Sometimes after the death of the parents, siblings begin to grow apart from each other. People get busy with their own lives, but I feel one should not let this happen. Siblings should be supportive to each other in a healthy way. It takes a mature and compassionate thinking, but it is possible.

Then there are some friends who give support and care in a time like this. Friends remind you about your wings when you are beginning to forget how to fly in depression. So be open and take support from friends. I was blessed to have support from a few friends who were angels in my grieving process. One friend in particular that I would like to thank helped my family and I deal with doctors and the hospital process. She was more knowledgeable about medicine than I was and she was able to help us understand what was going on. She has known my family for many years and I will never forget what she did for us. I will always be grateful to everyone who supported us through this time. I wish them health and happiness forever.

I have not spoken in detail about my brothers and sister in this book. Each family member has their own way of experiencing their own emotions, and I respect the privacy of my brothers and sister.

In the end, each of us, alone, as an individual, must live the journey and heal with it. I am very grateful to all my other family members for supporting me in their own ways.

VISIT TO INDIA, THE HEALING BEGINS

It's January 2006, A New Year, supposed to be new beginning. I have lost both my parents. My mother passed away in August 2004 and my father passed away a year later in 2005.

I have gained weight.

I have not come to terms with myself,

The effect of last two years is beginning to show on my face.

Emotionally I don't feel good.

But it's time. I must move on with my life.

I need a change of a scene.

I decided to go to India to visit my sister and her family, as well as my mother's relatives in Punjab. I also arranged to spend thirty-five days at an Ayurveda spa to rejuvenate my body and my mind. Hoping to melt away the stress and recharge my batteries. I arrived in India on January 29th, going first to Delhi.

***

My sister, Niru, came to pick me up at the airport.

Next day, her mother-in-law, 82 Years old, who had not been feeling well for a while, was admitted to the Hospital.

I went to see her with my sister. As I walked into the ICU room, she was lying with the oxygen mask on her face; it reminded me of my own mother.

I had an emotional outburst and tears.

I touched her feet, massaged her legs, just the way I used to do for my mother.

I put my hand on her forehead and prayed for her to have peace. Whatever that means.

After a while I left the room with tears, remembering how in the past whenever I saw her, she was always full of energy. Her first words used be 'Put jee (Son) has come. Oh, Niru your brother has come.'

This time she couldn't say anything, and didn't even know I was there.

VISIT TO TARA'S HOMETOWN

Two days later I went to Punjab to visit all my Mamaji's (my mother's brothers and family.) It was an emotional trip, visiting them for the first time after my parents had passed away. My parents had visited Punjab last time 3 years ago; that was their last trip to India. My parents used to come to India every 2 or 3 Years. All family members wanted to know the details of what happened with my mother while she was in the hospital. They expressed their sadness at not being able to visit so far away in America. They told me the last time when my mother left from there, she was looking at the house and them in a very special way and said she didn't know when she would come back again. She cried a lot like a child while saying good-bye to them as if she knew it was final. One of my Mamaji, Bhachan Das, cried a lot on the day of Rakhi (Sisters Day in India.) My Mami (Wife of Mama ji/ My Aunt) told me that.

I met three of my Mama ji, they all told me how much they missed my mother and father.

She was a very special sister to each one of them.

Each one confided in her, and she never told things about one to the other.

Each one of them said they missed her weekly phone calls from America.

Each one of them told stories about growing up with her as children.

All my cousins were very friendly with my father; they told me how much they remember him fondly.

***

In Punjab I also went to small village called 'Bhadhur.'

Bhadhur is the village where my mother was born and grew up. It's where the whole family used to live. Later three out of five Mamaji moved to another town, 'Bhatinda.'

I was also born in Bhadhur.

It is common in Indain culture for a woman who is about to give birth to a child to go back to her parents' house. That's why I was born in Bhadhur.

I stood silently with my eyes closed in the room where my mother gave birth to me.

***

Every summer during our school holidays, my mother would bring us to Bhadhur and Bhatinda, while my father would stay in Delhi taking care of his business. We used to be pampered and spoiled during the summer vacation. Those were the childhood days, a great memory.

One such memory comes to my mind. When I was 12 years old:

There is a river Bhadhur. My brother Chander and our cousins used to play and swim in the river. It was forbidden for us to go in that river because of the fear we might drown. But we still went in anyways. We used to take baths then dry our underwear and come home in the evening. One day somebody saw us and informed my mother that we were in the river.

"Were you playing in the river?" my mother asked in the evening when we came home.

"No," I lied.

"Show me your underwear," she said. She saw the underwear was dried but the string was not dried. She pointed that out and gave a slap on my face. "Son, don't do it again. It's not safe."

She was an intelligent mother throughout my whole life.

I remembered coming to Punjab for summer holidays, spending time with all my cousins. Even today it's the same loving experience whenever I come to Punjab. The time I spent there filled me with love, pure love.

This time I also noticed all my Mama jis have grown old. They are in their 70's; health is not 100% okay. It makes you think about the time when all our cousins were kids and all the Mama jis were young, running businesses. Today the cousins are grown up, married with kids. They have taken over the businesses and the Mama jis are old and semi-retired. It's also a wonderful feeling to see all cousins have grown up to be good people, successful and loving to their parents.

I said good-bye to all family members with tears full of joy and sadness.

One of my Mami ji, Sarala took me aside and said, "Your mother loved you very much. On many occasions she spoke about you to me. Tirlok Son, from now on, you take care of yourself and move forward in your life." She hugged me and blessed me with putting her hand on my head.

I hugged all my Mama jis and Mami jis for a long time. Touched their faces. Looked in their eyes. Kissed each one, both cheeks and forehead. Touched their feet. They blessed me by putting their hand on my head.

With the fear, knowing their age and physical condition, I wondered if I would see them again.

I left carrying with me much love …and I needed it.

***

In Punjab, I also went to see my father's sister Krishana in a town called Patialla. I hadn't seen her or her family for more than 20 years. We spoke about the last two years of the lives of my parents. I remember spending some of my childhood with her family. I felt bad that I had not seen her for so many years. It was healing experience.

ONE HUNDRED FUNERALS

On February 7th 2006, as I returned to Delhi, I was in the car coming from the station and my sister Niru called to inform me that her mother-in-law had just passed away a half an hour before. "The cremation will be in the evening."

As we drove towards the area for cremations, I could see the smoke from the pyres curling upwards into the heavens.

I joined the cremation process.

The dead body is placed on a six-foot long plank of wood with extended poles on four sides and then carried on shoulders from home to the cremation place. The sons, friends and other men in the family keep exchanging the burden on the way to cremation place. I joined in carrying the body on my shoulder as well. Once we reached the cremation place, we had to wait for our turn.

I saw an elevated platform.

Lying In the centre was a dead body.

A Hindu priest was reciting Mantras. A man - a relative of the person - was circling around the body carrying holy water called Ganga Jal (water from Gangas river) in a clay pot. He pours the Ganga jal from the pot as he circles around. At the last round, he breaks the clay pot by throwing it on the ground near the head of the dead body.

Then the dead body is removed and taken to cremation ground to be put on pyre of wood pieces.

The platform is cleaned with regular water.

Then it is our turn.

We do the same rituals, circling, throwing Ganga Jal, Mantras and Breaking the Pot.

As I witnessed the rituals, I felt the question surrounding us, who is next?

I turned around and saw there was somebody waiting to go next.

It's a line.

Is that what happens at God's Door in Heaven?

***

When we arrived at the cremation ground, I saw 11 pyres with dead bodies burning. There were holy mantras playing in the background.

There were groups of people around each pyre, totaling over 700 people.

Smoke was coming out of many pyres. Some pyres had no smoke but ashes were still red and hot. Some pyres were cool and the ashes looked white.

Up ahead, we walked to our designated pyre.

The body was placed on pyre of woods.

A Hindu priest uncovered the face of the body.

It was the last look, never to be seen again in her physical form.

Face was covered. Many many wood pieces were put upon and around her body. More Mantras were read and prayers were spoken.

Then my sister's husband R.P. and his brother Narinder circled around the body and lit the fire. (In the Hindu tradition it is always the elder son or the sons who light the fire.)

In few minutes pyre starts to burn fully. People gather around and watch.

I looked at the faces of the family.

I felt compassion for all of them. I knew, very well, how it felt. I knew that at this moment they were in shock. They would only begin to feel the impact more deeply in days to come.

I prayed for the peace of everyone present at that cremation ground.

I moved from one pyre to another, joining in the grief of each group.

Standing amidst the burning pyres of bodies in their final moments I could see the bigger picture of death and life.

I came back to the pyre of our family member. The pyre was burning full blaze.

I looked right into it. I knew the person very well under that pyre. I have many good memories of her from over the years. She has been a good woman and had lived a good life.

***

An incident from when I was 10 came to mind.

We were living as a joint family on Sadar Thana Road in Delhi. One day I was standing in the balcony of the house and I noticed a dead body being carried in the street. A band was playing, marching ahead in front of the Dead Body procession. My mother and grandmother were also there on the balcony.

"Why is the band marching? Why is the person wrapped in that red cloth?" I asked.

"The red cloth means it's a woman," my grandmother replied. "For a man it will be white cloth. The band is playing music. That means she has lived a full life and she is an aged woman. She has completed her life in this world. Her life is a celebration. So her death and leaving this world, going to heaven is also Celebration."

***

Now, standing in the middle of cremation ground as a grown man, I reminded myself: if people have lived a good life, when they die, it should be a celebration of life.

Everyone present had witnessed the burning of a body of a person they knew, maybe a loved one, or a family member. They will go home tonight, each person affected to the extent of their relationship with the dead one.

They will change their clothes and take a shower or bath, to wash away the effects and presence of being at a cremation. It is an Indian tradition to wash after going to a cremation.

Some of them will never be able to wash away the grief they have, no matter how many baths or showers they take, especially the ones who have just lost their mother or father.

As we left, I looked back up at the entrance. There was a 50 foot high beautiful colorful statue of Lord Shiva - The Destroyer (according to Hindu mythology.) I also saw an inscription on the door: "Moksh Dawar" (A Door to the Salvation.)

I went home, took a bath but could not wash away the effects of witnessing the cremation of the lady I had known for 30+ years. I felt compassion for the family and I prayed to God to bless them with the Peace and Strength to accept life. I knew this feeling very well, as I was also thinking about my parents.

ONE HUNDRED MASSAGES

The next day, February 8th 2006, I went to Calicut, Kerala for 35 days.

I came to Calicut for an Ayurvedic Rejuvenation spa, to take care of my body, hoping to melt away the stress and sadness.

My notes from this time of Ayurvedic healing:

I am here for health.

I get very tired; it's a process of cleansing the body.

I am advised to relax and get well.

I get massages everyday.

The first week, two people give me massages using all the Ayurvedic Herbal oils.

Sometimes three or six people at a time give me a massage depending upon the treatment.

The massage therapists are very caring. My body can feel that.

I am given a specific kind and amount of food.

I have a room on the 4th floor, Room No. 401, overlooking palm trees. Many of them. Green. Standing tall.

When I sit near the window, I see the top of a tree that is very close to my window.

I look at it many times while sipping cumin spiced hot water.

A little further away, I can see ocean meeting the sky.

I can also see earth.

I see many birds flying in sky, some solo, some in the company of others.

It is a peaceful view for me.

***

The next morning, the General Manager of the Spa joins me while I was having my breakfast in the coffee shop.

After the formal talk, he started telling me about his mother. She died at age of 52, while he was only 22 years old.

Three days before she died he spoke to her when he gotten his first job in a major hotel in Bombay. His first paycheck was for 325 Rupees. He sent a money order of 275 rupees to his mother.

She never got the money order; she passed away a day before it reached her.

After 30 years he still feels regret.

Listening to this, I had tears in my eyes.

Seeing me, he let his emotions go and cried as well.

I got up and gave him hug, saying, "This is from your mother."

He stood embracing me tight in the middle of Coffee Shop.

A beautiful moment – we are so fortunate when we can feel.

***

On my last two trips to the Ayurveda Spa, I often called my parents in New York to say Hello. It was a pleasure speaking to them. My mother always blessed me with good health. This time they are not there to answer my call. But I am sure they are still wishing me good health.

So I am healing myself here. Some days I feel better than others. I intend to come to terms with my life's recent happenings and move forward.

HOLI TO HARIDAWAR

On March 14th 2006, I came back to Delhi to my sister's home. We celebrated the festival called "Holi." It's a festival of colors. People sprinkle colors on each other, eat sweets and celebrate the victory of believing in the power of good over evil. I remembered as a kid it used to be lot of fun to play Holi.

During the week of March 20th to 28th 2006, I went to Haridawar. Haridawar is a holy city according to Hindus. People go there bathe in the holy river, to receive blessings from God like a pilgrim. Haridawar literally means Dwar to Hari (Gateway to God). Many people also go there to put ashes in the river after the cremation because of the Hindu Faith in the Gateway to Heaven.

I accompanied a family who had just lost their daughter. They came from the United States, Chicago, to put ashes in the river of their recently deceased young twenty-year old daughter. She had caught a virus and died within a few hours. She was living in a hostel near the college campus where she was studying. I had met her when she came to New York three years ago. She was full of life and had an infectious energy. She loved to dance. I felt sad upon getting the news of her untimely death. I can imagine it must be one of the most horrible experiences for a parent to see the death of their child.

When a young life that has not yet been fully lived is taken away, it is natural to question why. Her parents had so much love and faith for their daughter's future and then all of sudden the child was gone…

The universe has presented me with another example about the bigger picture of life and death. After witnessing this, it became a part my healing process.

***

While I was in Delhi, I visited the school where I studied as a child. I went to the house on Sadar Thana Road where I grew up. Looking down, I stood on the very same balcony where at the age of 10 I had a conversation with my grandmother about the old lady, the red cloth and the band.

***

A CHECK LIST

After visiting with my family in India and reflecting on experiences I had, I made a checklist of my thoughts about my parents, and the list is as follows:

LIFE FULLY LIVED IS A CELEBRATION

And yes indeed my parents lived a full life.

My parents lived life with integrity as good human beings.

They were good parents to us children.

They loved each other for sixty years.

They were good friends to their friends.

They contributed to the society no matter where they lived.

They were good citizens of the world.

They were good family members to their relatives.

They were kind, generous, caring and compassionate.

They may not have been 100% perfect but they were great human beings.

Did they feel accomplished when they left this world?

Yes they did, as they told me many times before they passed away.

It's not important how one dies, it's how one lived.

I salute them and feel lucky to be their child.

***

We want our parents and loved ones to live forever, even though God has not designed the human body that way. I will never again be able to see my parents in a physical manner.

I will begin to connect with them in a spiritual way, so that I can feel them around, can talk to them whenever I wish to. I will set up my own special way to communicate with them.

What happens to a soul when a person dies? According to Hindu Mythology when a person dies their soul goes to a place called "Brahmmand."

All souls rest in Brahmmand. They meet other souls of the people they have known in their lives on the earth. They finish any unfinished attachments with the people they have left behind. It is also said that we people who are left behind on earth by our loved ones, should set the departed souls free so that they can rest in peace. That's why it is said, may God bless the deceased soul to rest in peace. Souls that are in a limbo, having attachments on the earth, are not in peace. Once the soul has rested fully and the time has come to be reborn, the Creator gives them rebirth. It is also said the souls who are super-enlightened or have come to salvation can become angels and live forever in the company of the Creator. One should be free from all "Maya" connections when they leave the Earth. That would be the ideal life.

My parents were very spiritual people, lived full life. They left this world fully content, free from all Maya Connections and are now in Brahmmand. They must have connected with each other in Brahmmand. Their souls are resting in peace.

That's what I like to believe.

In spite of all my sadness of losing them, I must set them free emotionally. I must come to terms.

I can always think of them with love.

I can miss them on many occasions.

I can remember all the wonderful memories.

I can remember them with some sad memories as well.

But I must move on with my life with happiness, even though it will be very hard at times.

And at those times I should forgive myself but keep on trying. That's what would make my parents happy.

BACK IN NEW YORK

I'm standing in the middle of my parent's apartment. Nothing has been touched since my father passed away in August 2005. I've tried a few times before to clean out the place but somehow how I just couldn't. Maybe it was my way of keeping them alive.

But now I am prepared and ready to deal with it. My brother Chandler and a friend Deva were there to help me during this time. We took most of their clothing and other things to Salvation Army or a Church close by. We also kept a few mementos for ourselves.

While moving boxes, an incident that happened five years ago in that apartment came to mind:

One evening while I was having a conversation with my parents in their apartment, my mother said, "You should be living happily and smiling - that's how I want to leave this world" (Tumko hasthe Khelthe chodhke jahun). I hit my mother lightly on her arm and said, "Why you are talking like this?" (Bibi, Thu kuin Aase bolthe hai.) "Son," she said, "I have lived a good life. There is a big line at God's home. Everybody has to go one day. (Meri zindagi changi rahi hain, rub the kar lambi line hai, sabko ek din janahi hain.)" I said to her "Whatever, don't talk like that"(jo kuch bhi hain, astra gal na kar). I put my arms around her. She touched my face.

Yes, everyone has to go one day but I wish you could have stayed longer.

Yes, I will do my best to live your wish but just remember there will be times when I will miss you so much that I may feel sad. And at those times I will just say to the cosmic universe that I love you forever. I will always remember your touch of August 1st 2004 when you touched my jaw to make me smile. That touch sealed in me for my whole lifetime your unconditional love. I hope you met father in Brahmmand. Please tell him I will always treasure the last day we spent together. I will always remember my last words to him, "I love you" and his last words to me "I love you too."

I love you both forever. Your son, Tirlok

A NOTE ON HOSPITALS

Here I would like to share some of my thoughts about hospitals and rehab centers:

In the hospital, my parents were taken care of by nurses from many countries such as America, Africa, South America, Spain, Philippines, Guyana, India, Poland, England and others. She also had male nurses. Hospitals in New York are truly multicultural. I found from my experience when it came to taking care of a patient, we are one universal people whether we are giving care or receiving.

In the Indian tradition when a patient and the patient's family looks at a doctor, the doctor represents the image of a semi-God who might be able to save and cure the patient. This is how I felt about doctors who were treating my mother. I use to fold my hands (a gesture of Indian way to thank) to greet her doctors and thank them for taking care of my mother. Further I would say, "I and my family are grateful to you; we pray for the well being of your family". I meant it a million times more than words could say. My impression and feeling about doctors has changed because of the experience I had dealing with them. We cannot trust their judgment all the time. They do make mistakes. I thought they were never supposed to make mistakes but they do. Sometimes it could be an honest mistake and sometimes it's because they are not doing their work with 100% responsibility. Sometimes it is about the 'bottom line.' One must be aware when dealing with doctors that we should not have blind faith in them. At the same time, let them do their work. Regardless, I am grateful to those doctors and health workers who did their work with compassion and professionalism.

My thoughts for Doctors, Nurses, Social Workers, Health Workers:

> **A patient is one person to you in the world. But please remember:**
>
> **One patient is the world to somebody,**
>
> **Be compassionate,**
>
> **Do not take your work just as a job,**
>
> **Try to feel you are contributing a priceless service, which cannot be valued in money.**
>
> **It is your contribution to humanity.**

When you are visiting hospital for long time either for yourself or someone you know is there, you begin to observe and learn many good and bad things about the medical process.

Sometimes you are very surprised to make your discoveries. Sometimes you learn the hospital is not operated the way you think it is - or should be - operated.

It can be very stressful. Yes hospitals are good. We need them to take care of patients. Sometimes it will make you frustrated and angry. Sometimes you feel grateful. All sorts of people work in the hospital. They vary in nature. Some of them are more caring, and compassionate than others. For some it's just a job. For some it's a job *and* a noble profession. Some think it's just work and get paid. Some think its job *and* they are making a contribution to patients' well being. You will also find in dealing with some people that they should not work in this profession.

Some people are able to bring only compassion and professionalism to hospital when they enter to start their shift. Some bring their personal problems or personality problems along when they enter into Hospital to start their shift. But when you yourself or someone you love is in the hospital and expects compassion and professional service, when it is not given, you will be shocked, frustrated and angry. You feel let down. Sometimes you also feel grateful when it is given. I felt all these feelings with my experience in dealing with the hospitals, rehab centers, doctors, social workers and nurses. At the same time, I also met some very compassionate and professional people in this field.

Some of the things one may experience:

- Hospitals are operated with the motive of Wall Street or it is part of Wall Street. This was told to me by an in charge of Administration at the Hospital. I also felt this at times in my experience.

- Doctors and medical staff make decisions based on a paper trail. What that means: doctors, who may do a procedure on a patient, will see the patient for the first time in Operation Room. They are only looking at the comments made by the previous medical staff, before the case comes to them. Hopefully you will be lucky that any one along the way made no wrong diagnosis. I experienced this in my mother's case.

- Sometimes you are faced with a conflict when things go wrong - was it a human error or destiny of the patient? How do you resolve the situation if you are faced with this conflict?

- Sometimes you won't believe the insensitive nature of health workers.

Doctors always seem to be in rush. They may be overworked or have too many patients. Many times you wish a doctor would take the time to explain things to you in layman's language. So you can easily understand if you are not a very medically informed person.

Ayurveda Café – A Place for Balance, A Mother's Kitchen

It's an Indian vegetarian restaurant on 94th Street and Amsterdam Avenue in New York City (www.theAyurvedaCafe.com), serving healthy food. It does not have a traditional menu. It's a pre-fixe meal of the day. And that is what is cooked and served to all the visitors to Ayurveda Café. In 1998, I had finished studying Ayurveda. It was a time when I wanted more spiritual Ayurvedic understanding in my life. In conversation with my brother Chander Malik, it was decided that Ayurveda Café would be opened for our mother, Tara. She was a vegetarian and we thought it would be nice to have a place where my parents could "hang out" and where other people could also enjoy the same spiritual experience of food.

Ayurveda Café is just like going to a mother's kitchen where you don't ask what you want to eat. You enjoy what is being cooked and served. It has been a very successful concept.

We opened Ayurveda Café for her and for everyone else who will visit the Café. When we told our mother and father we were opening the restaurant for them, my mother had tears in her eyes. When the restaurant was opened, she lit the first fire to cook the first meal. She was very proud of that place.

Ayurveda Café is not a place just for food. It's an experience. When you walk in, you surrender to whatever will be served to you. The place itself combines sound, music, color and aromatherapy to create the effect of relaxation. When visitors to the Café leave, they leave smiling and contented with the experience. As a matter of fact, Ayurveda Café proposes a guaranty - if you do not leave satisfied, you do not pay. This place is truly for body, mind and soul. There's an invisible energy, which can only come from a loving mother like Tara.

My brother Chander is one of the best restaurateurs I have known and worked with. I remember the early times in our career. We were working in a coffee shop on 49th Street and Eighth Avenue. He was the cook and I worked as the waiter. It was a tourist neighborhood. Chander would cook from 7 AM to 11 AM almost two hundred breakfasts. I would only speak the order; he would listen without any paperwork; he would remember whose plate had whole-wheat toast or rye toast. It was amazing to watch him. As a restauranteur, he has developed concept restaurants and turned them into brands known and respected in New York City. He's a great host. You meet him once, and you will remember him – unforgettable.

Ayurveda Café has been a healthy place for me. I can still feel my parents' presence there. It's like a temple to Tara and Amrit. I would like to share some of the incidents from the Ayurveda Café:

We had only been open one week when two customers said to me, "You will never survive here because you are telling people what to eat." I said, "We are not telling people what to eat. We are telling them what we are serving. People have a choice because the menu is written on the board outside." Then I asked, "By the way, are you guys therapists?" They said, "Yes, but how do you know?" I said, "Because therapy does not understand the concept of surrender. And this place is about surrendering to the experience." They became regular customers after that.

***

One day an Indian taxi driver came in for dinner. After the dinner he said, "I was very hungry. I was driving by. I saw an empty parking space outside the Ayurveda Café so I came in. After I had the food, it reminded me of my mother." He became very emotional. It was a great compliment.

***

I was speaking to a couple who had been married for two years. They always celebrated the anniversary of their first date at the Ayurveda Café. The man told me when he was going to take her out on a date he wanted to take her to the best vegetarian restaurant. When he searched, he read about the Ayurveda Café - a lot more than just the food. It became "their place" and they got married.

***

Now, every Mother's and Father's Day, if any visitor brings in their mother or father, we give them a complimentary meal - as a celebration of all parents.

***

Until 2003, my mother and father always sat in the corner table at a 45-degree angle so they could see all the visitors and wave. They were proud of this restaurant and most visitors knew them as our parents.

***

Once we had a waitress who, on her first day, was crying in the back of the restaurant. When asked what happened, she said, "Your mother made me cry." I asked "Why?" She had worn a top showing a little cleavage. My mother sat her down and told her, "What is this? Close the button." Then the waitress said, "It reminded me of my own mother. She was the only one who would have dared to tell me that. And I became very emotional. I'm not angry with your mother. It just made me miss my own mother."

***

Our chef at Ayurveda Café is a dear lady who does not need to work and is a mother herself – and a grandmother. She comes in every day, begins with a prayer to the universe, and then cooks the food with love. My mother, who was a great cook as well, loved her cooking.

***

Every year on my birthday and on my brother's birthday, my mother would give a gift of money to all the workers and say, "Buy something you'd like." Afterwards the workers would all wish my brother or I a very happy birthday. We'd ask how they all knew that today was our birthday and we found out that our mother had given each employee $10-20.

***

Ayurveda Café nurtures the mind as well as the spirit and body. There's an antique Indian box full of slips of paper, each with a short message of wisdom. Each customer, when leaving, chooses a message from the box without first reading it. Most customers tell us they received a message for which they needed to hear on that particular day. Customers call it the magic box and somehow, someway this magic seems to work… I think I can guess who is working the magic, because Ayurveda. Café is the temple of Tara and Amrit.

Khushiyaan, the Film

Khushiyaan is a film about a family's journey when they are faced with the reality of life – and someone they love is going to die. [www.KhushiyaanTheFilm.com]

While living in America, I saw many Indian Americans whose parents are living in India while they live in the US. And one day they get the news that one of their parents has died. I have witnessed the effect of this news people who feel frustrated, angry and sad all at once because they realize they did not spend enough time with their parents, or they were not there while their parents were dying. It made me sad a number of times when I witnessed that.

I always advocated that one must spend time with their parents while they are healthy and living. Our life is very busy. We all know that. But we need to make time.

I've been to funerals of my friends' parents. I always felt bad when I was at the funerals, but I never knew how deeply it would hurt until it happened to me. So after the death of my parents, I wanted to share the message: spend time with your parents while they're alive. So that once the parents are gone, at least you have that satisfaction deep in your heart that you have stored enough memories so that you will be able to live on in peace after they have died. How could I share this message? I am a filmmaker. I have been making films for many years (www.nritvfilmclub.com) and I'm lucky enough to have done some good work, including a New York Emmy award nomination. Because of this, I felt it would be a very good story to tell through a film.

My film was inspired by the love story of my parents. It has a positive message because in the film the son who lives in America goes to India to visit his parents for something else. While there, he discovers his father is dying from cancer. He invites his own son and wife to India to spent time with his parents. The whole family collectively goes through the experience and the journey of coming to terms with the fact that the father is going to die. But the film is not about death; it is about the celebration of life.

If you're aware that you will one day lose your parents and all your loved ones, it's a reality you cannot change; but you can change how you will feel after they have gone if you have spent time with them and have memories to live on.

Khushiyaan, the moments of happiness, was shot in New York and India. It was an interesting experience working in both countries. It was my first time making a film in

India after making several in the U.S. One of the biggest distribution companies in Indian entertainment, Eros International distributed the film worldwide.

The film was well received by many. They liked the message I had to say in the film. Many audience members sent me emails congratulating me for making a film on such a beautiful theme that touched their heart and reminded them of the value of the family. Some people even made small donations through my website after watching the film. And more than a million people saw the film on bootleg copies and downloaded the free music thanks to global Internet piracy.

I feel my producers and I will leave something behind that will touch people's hearts, even after we all are gone.

A GIFT

My parents always wanted me to be with a life partner who would be as loving, caring and supportive to me as they were to each other. Sometime after my parents passed away, a lovely, caring, and beautiful woman came into my life.

She is a gift from my parents.

IF TODAY WAS YOUR LAST DAY

Most of the times we don't tell people what our heart really says because we fear their reaction.

I invite you the reader; write a letter to yourself where you say what you would say to the people in your life, if it were your last day on earth. Discover for yourself.

_____,

_____

_____

_____

_____

_____

_____

_____

_____

_____

_____

_____

_____

_____

_____

Tirlok Malik, Filmmaker, Actor, Restauranteur.

Tirlok Malik is a New York Emmy Award nominated filmmaker. Tirlok was born in India and now lives in New York City. He has produced many films since 1990 starting with his first pioneer film about Indian American experiences, "Lonely in America." The film was shown in 74 countries and participated in 37 film festivals, winning many Awards.

As an Actor he has acted in many television series, and films. He has also acted onstage in over 200 performances in New York City. He has appeared in many television and print commercials for mainstream US television. He has also worked with many big starts from the Indian Film Industry such as Rajinikanth, Kamal Haasan, Surya, Sanjay Dutt, Mammootty, Sunny Deol, Kangana Ranaut and many more.

Tirlok Malik's award winning film "KHUSHIYAAN" (moments of happiness) was shot in New York and India. The film was inspired by this memoir.

Tirlok Malik's new film is dealing with what if this is your last Valentine day with your partner. Title "On Golden Years." It takes place in a only Indian retirement community in America called Shantiniketan in Florida.

Tirlok Malik and his brother Chander Malik are the co-founders of Ayurveda Café on 94th and Amsterdam Avenue in New York City. They opened the restaurant in the spirit of their mother's kitchen, a homely peaceful place for people to eat healthy vegetarian Indian food. www.theayurvedecafe.com

Tirlok Malik is also the founder of the NRI TV Film Club. This production company continues to nurture multicultural new talent in films and television. www.nritvfilmclub.com

He can be reached at applecasting@gmail.com